More praise for

First Principles

"A veteran policy maker and exceptional economist, John B. Taylor gives us the guiding ideas we need to get back to prosperity without inflation, and he does so in clear, compelling, and readable prose."   —George P. Shultz, former Secretary of State

"Taylor has long advanced bold reforms that apply our nation's timeless principles to the challenges of today. Taylor's latest contribution to the national debate could not come at a more important moment. *First Principles* is an important guide for policymakers and the citizens we serve."   —U.S. Congressman Paul Ryan

"John Taylor argues persuasively for a return to the founding principles of our free society—rule of law, predictable government policies, and free markets—and shows how violation of these principles has derailed American prosperity time and again. This book sends a clear and powerful message to everyone searching for a way out of the malaise gripping the nation." —Gary Becker, University of Chicago, winner of the Nobel Prize in Economics

"All political candidates . . . should read Stanford University economist John Taylor's new book, *First Principles*. . . . Remarkably readable and convincing." —*City Journal*

"Every time John Taylor writes a book, it's an important book. . . . A man of great insight and great erudition." —Dr. Edwin Feulner, president of the Heritage Foundation

"This book is readable, short, focused. . . . I can't say enough about it." —Tom Keene, on Bloomberg Television's "Surveillance Midday"

"Thought-provoking." —*Financial Review of Books*

"If policy makers had followed Taylor's principles, we'd probably be a lot better off than we are today. . . . Taylor has written an excellent guide for policy going forward." —Bill Watkins, Center for Economic Research and Forecasting

"The book is readable, fascinating, useful and important. It deserves to be widely read and to have its advice widely followed." —Geoffrey Wood, *Central Banking Journal*

"I am often asked for recommendations of easy-to-read books that illuminate modern macroeconomics. . . . This book belongs high on the list. . . . It is clear, accessible, measured, and concise." —John Cochrane, Senior Fellow at the Hoover Institution

First
Principles

∎ ∎ ∎ ∎ ∎

Also by John B. Taylor

Ending Government Bailouts As We Know Them
(with Kenneth E. Scott and George P. Shultz)

The Road Ahead for the Fed
(with John D. Ciorciari)

Getting Off Track:
How Government Actions and Interventions Caused, Prolonged, and
Worsened the Financial Crisis

Global Financial Warriors:
The Untold Story of International Finance in the Post-9/11 World

Monetary Policy Rules

Handbook of Macroeconomics
(with Michael Woodford)

Inflation, Unemployment, and Monetary Policy
(with Robert M. Solow)

Principles of Economics
(with Akila Weerapana)

Macroeconomic Policy in a World Economy:
From Econometric Design to Practical Operation

Macroeconomics: Theory, Performance, and Policy
(with Robert E. Hall)

First Principles

Five Keys to Restoring America's Prosperity

John B. Taylor

W. W. NORTON & COMPANY

New York • London

To Olivia and Andrew

For information about permission to reproduce selections from this book,
write to Permissions, W. W. Norton & Company, Inc.,
500 Fifth Avenue, New York, NY 10110

For information about special discounts for bulk purchases, please contact
W. W. Norton Special Sales at specialsales@wwnorton.com or 800-233-4830

Manufacturing by Courier Westford
Book design by Chris Welch Design
Production manager: Julia Druskin

Library of Congress Cataloging-in-Publication Data

Taylor, John B.
First principles : five keys to restoring America's prosperity /
John B. Taylor. — 1st ed.
p. cm.
Includes bibliographical references and index.
ISBN 978-0-393-07339-3 (hardcover)
1. Monetary policy—United States. 2. United States—Economic policy—
21st century. 3. United States—Politics and government—21st century. I. Title.
HG230.3.T395 2012
339.50973—dc23

2011048147

ISBN 978-0-393-34545-2 pbk.

W. W. Norton & Company, Inc.
500 Fifth Avenue, New York, N.Y. 10110
www.wwnorton.com

W. W. Norton & Company Ltd.
Castle House, 75/76 Wells Street, London W1T 3QT

Contents

Preface to the Paperback Edition

In the year since this book first went to press, the principles of economic freedom have not, of course, changed. At its most basic level, economic freedom means that people are free to decide what to produce, what to consume, what to buy and sell, and how to help others within the context of predictable government policy based on the rule of law with strong incentives derived from the market system and with a clearly limited role for government. I wrote this book because I was concerned that America was drifting away from these principles, and, as a result, the American economy was in trouble.

While one year spans only a short slice of history, the events of the past year greatly reinforce these concerns and show that the obstacles to restoring America's prosperity are more formidable than ever.

The fiscal cliff of expiring temporary tax cuts and other measures, which completely dominated the economic and political scene in Washington at year-end 2012, vividly illustrates the harm of deviating from predictable policy. The fiscal cliff was not created by aliens from outer space. It was the culmination of many short-term-oriented policy decisions over the past few years, which have created uncertainty and held back investment and hiring—as I stress in the book.

In the meantime, more evidence on the ground bolsters many other facts reported in the book. A fourth straight annual trillion dollar deficit in 2012 added to the sharply rising federal debt. Indeed, the debt explosion illustrated on page 102 so scared the people at the Congressional Budget Office that they stopped reporting the bad news as if that would make it go away. Washington politicians have made little progress in reducing the federal government spending binge illustrated on page 113, and they even backtracked on agreements made last year. We now know that the Federal Reserve bought a whopping 77 percent of the increased debt in 2011, and Fed decisions made in 2012 will so expand its unpredictable and intrusive quantitative easing that the alarming line on page 140 will jump right through the top of the page.

And the explosion of entitlements growth illustrated on page 170 has not been addressed.

So it is not surprising that the economic growth slowed in 2012—to only half what the Federal Reserve had forecast as recently as 2011. The percentage of the population with a job remains well below what it was before the 2007–2009 recession, and long-term unemployment continues at record levels.

More than ever, America needs the type of comprehensive budget, tax, monetary, and regulatory reform plan outlined in the book.

Yet the obstacles remain high. Many are making the case that all America has to do is raise taxes on the rich or regulations on entrepreneurs or fiscal and monetary stimulus interventions and prosperity will improve. Others are buying the arguments that incentives and the rule of law do not matter or that well-intentioned government activism beats the market any day. Ironically, reformers in China and other emerging markets are telling the story of economic freedom as they move away from central planning and their economies grow rapidly bringing hundreds of millions of people out of poverty. While China has been bringing people out of poverty, America has been putting more people into poverty. Adherence to the principles of economic freedom is the surest way to improve the lot of all Americans.

The awarding of the 2012 Hayek Prize and the general positive response to *First Principles* means that people are becoming interested in these ideas and the broad benefits they bring not only for the middle class and but also for the poor and disadvantaged. Highly taxed or excessively regulated firms scared off by unpredictable government controls on their prices and products are reluctant to expand or create jobs; thus unemployment remains high. Children in poor neighborhoods prevented by government rules from going to good schools and learning needed skills will be trapped into high unemployment or low wages, and income inequality will persist across generations. And the principles of economic freedom will provide more growth and thereby more resources for needed infrastructure and other public goods.

Understanding that our economic problems are caused largely by government policies that have deviated from the principles of economic freedom is the first step to bringing about a change in policy and thereby restoring prosperity.

John B. Taylor
December 2012

Preface

This book presents a strategy for restoring the greatness of the American economy. The strategy is based on nothing more than the principles of economic freedom upon which the country was founded.

I begin in chapter 1 by describing these first principles and showing how adherence to them has ebbed and flowed over the years, creating waves of bad economic times and good economic times. The clear implication is that our current economic problems are caused by a deviation from these principles, and thus the key to restoring greatness is to restore these great principles.

To help understand these ebbs and flows, in chapter 2

I delve into the decision-making process in Washington, identifying key policymakers who stuck to, ignored, or compromised on the principles; drawing lessons from their mistakes and successes; and tracing connections over time. Neither political party wholly owns the successes or the mistakes.

In the remaining chapters of the book I then show how to apply these principles to crucial economic policy areas—fiscal policy, monetary policy, regulation, entitlements, and the global economy. The result is a comprehensive economic strategy based on proven economic principles that have worked in the past and will work in the future.

This book has three antecedents. First is my research on monetary and fiscal policy rules, which I began to pursue in the 1960s. That research predicted that economic performance could be improved greatly if monetary and fiscal policy followed certain well-defined economic principles; the prediction was borne out by much better economic performance in the 1980s and 1990s compared with that of the late 1960s and 1970s.

The second antecedent is my book on the 2008 financial crisis, *Getting Off Track: How Government Actions Caused, Prolonged, and Worsened the Financial Crisis*. That book, written in the midst of the panic in the fall of 2008, was one of the first on the financial crisis. I examined the facts and the policy decisions. I found that deviations from the same basic economic principles led to the crisis and that if policymakers had not deviated from these principles, we would have avoided the crisis. Since then I have done additional empirical research which shows that if policymakers had returned to these principles after the crisis, then they would have handled the ensuing recession and the economic recovery much better.

I've read books and articles that blame the crisis, the recession, and the weak recovery on the failure of the market system or the failure of economics. I've listened to speeches by policymakers defending their policy decisions, claiming that the economy would have been even worse if policy had not deviated from these economic principles. Such views are off base and would lead us astray. I am writing this book to remind people what the principles are and why they work, so we can get back on track.

The third antecedent is my book *Global Financial Warriors: The Untold Story of International Finance in the Post-9/11 World*, in which I endeavored to explain how to apply economic principles in practice, using my experience directing the international division of the U.S. Treasury in the years after 9/11. This book expands on that experience, drawing on my other stints in Washington, interviewing others who served at different times, and going beyond international financial policy to the full

range of policy issues America confronts today. Knowing
the principles is not enough. We've got to know how to
follow and implement them and ward off many pressures
to deviate from them.

In writing this book, I stand on the shoulders of economic giants, including Milton Friedman, whose book
Capitalism and Freedom was published in the same year
that a new interventionist wave hit American economic
policy with the persuasive 1962 *Economic Report of the
President*, written by such distinguished economists as
Walter Heller, James Tobin, and Kermit Gordon when
they served on President John Kennedy's Council of Economic Advisers. As George Shultz, another economic
giant engaged in the political arena, said when he served
as Secretary of the Treasury in 1973, "Economists have a
particular responsibility to relate policy decisions to the
maintenance of freedom, so that when the combination
of special interest groups, bureaucratic pressures, and congressional appetites calls for still one more increment of
government intervention, we can calculate the cost in
these terms." We have learned much more about how
the principles of freedom should inform economic policy
decisions in the nearly half century since then.

I want to thank my colleagues in the Economics
Department at Stanford University and in the Working
Group on Economic Policy at Stanford's Hoover Institu-

tion for many discussions on these issues. Much of this book is based on joint research and writing collaborations with Scott Atlas, Gary Becker, Michael Boskin, John Cogan, Allan Meltzer, Dan Kessler, Ken Scott, George Shultz, Johannes Stroebel, John Williams, and Frank Wolak. I am also grateful to Don Lamm, who encouraged me to write the book, and to Drake McFeely and Brendan Curry, who encouraged me to bring the ideas together into a coherent theme and provided extraordinary editorial advice as I wrote.

1

First Principles Work

America's economic future is uncertain. The financial crisis of 2008, the deep recession that followed it, and now anemic economic growth and high unemployment are obvious signs of an economy in trouble. This is not the economy that most Americans had come to expect from the more prosperous decades of the twentieth century. Rather it looks like a rerun of the 1970s, or even worse, the 1930s, when unemployment was high and economic growth was low. The worry now is that such poor performing decades will become the norm of the twenty-first century, with disastrous consequences for future generations and diminished American leadership in the world.

Some people say that the financial crisis and the deep recession were caused by inherent failures of the market system, or at least by too much reliance on that system. But the facts and timing readily available in the historical record show that certain government actions and interventions that preceded the crisis are a much more probable cause, as I showed in my book *Getting Off Track* and as I build on in this book.

When the recovery from the deep recession turned out to be very weak, many of the same people continued to blame inherent economic weaknesses rather than government policy, pointing to the long time needed for the economy to recover as people cut back on consumption and paid back debt. However, the economic recovery wasn't nearly so weak in the early 1980s following back-to-back recessions and higher unemployment, even though people consumed a much smaller fraction of their income in that recovery. Instead strong economic growth caused unemployment to fall rapidly. And while housing has been weak in recent years, all strong economies have weak sectors, and housing is less of a drag now than other sectors, such as foreign trade, were in the strong 1980s recovery. The problems with today's economy are neither inherent weaknesses nor new intractable factors that have turned against it.

The First Principles

The premise of this book is that the best way to understand the problems confronting the American economy is to go back to the first principles of economic freedom upon which the country was founded. As these principles developed over the years, we can see periods when careful attention was paid to them and alternating periods when they were neglected. And we can draw clear conclusions from this history: When policymakers stuck to the principles, economic performance was good. When they ignored or compromised on the principles, economic performance deteriorated.

Our problem now is that we are paying too little attention to these principles, and even worse, we are moving in the wrong direction. The good news is that if we begin to apply these principles to our current circumstances, we can restore America's prosperity and our confidence in the future.

At its most basic level, economic freedom means that families, individuals, and entrepreneurs are free to decide what to produce, what to consume, what to buy and sell, and how to help others. The American vision was that those decisions would be made within a *predictable* government policy framework based on the *rule of law* with strong *incentives* derived from the *market* system and with a clearly *limited role for government*.

The principles of economic freedom are naturally intertwined with political freedom—speech, press, assembly, religion. Excessive government interventions and economic controls will tend to constrain people's freedom to speak out or take public political positions for fear of retribution through more interventions and controls. The loss of political freedom can in turn reduce economic freedom further.

One of the most amazing things about these defining principles of economic freedom

- predictable policy framework
- rule of law
- strong incentives
- reliance on markets
- clearly limited role for government

is that they also constitute a set of principles for economic success. Economic theory and experience show that they lead to superior economic outcomes, including strong economic growth and rising prosperity. The principles of liberty that Thomas Jefferson and the other founding fathers first delineated in the Declaration of Independence in 1776 are remarkably similar to the principles of economics that Adam Smith first heralded in the *Wealth of Nations* in the same year, and that remain central to economics today.

Markets, incentives, and a carefully delineated role for government are the main pillars of basic economics courses and texts, including the introductory course I've taught college students for years and my textbook *Principles of Economics*. In a market economy, most decisions about what to produce, how to produce it, and for whom it is produced are made by individuals, firms, and organizations interacting in markets. Prices in those markets signal what goods and services people want, and the prices create incentives to produce those goods and services. For instance, a greater demand for healthy foods increases their price and thereby gives firms the incentive to produce more healthy foods. The higher price also provides incentives to people to invent new healthier (and perhaps even tastier) foods and to create firms to sell the new products.

The higher wages paid for skilled labor offer people the incentive to become skilled, whether by staying in school or by learning on the job. As they respond to these incentives, people who become more skilled are frequently led by Adam Smith's "invisible hand to promote" the interests of society through more effective medicines, more entertaining movies, or more efficient search engines. When greater economic freedom increases opportunities to trade at home and abroad, the existing incentives expand and economic prosperity increases. Lower income tax rates increase incentives by raising the benefits (higher incomes) one gets from investing in education or a start-up business.

The foundational economic principles recognize a role for government in providing public goods such as national defense, maintaining the environment, protecting individual rights and liberties, and creating a social safety net for those who are poor or disabled. But when assigning these and other roles to government, we must clearly define their extent, we must take into account both benefits and costs, and we must explain the case for a government role rather than a market-based solution. We must also recognize that government programs can fail, sometimes because they give power to people who favor entrenched interests. Indeed, Adam Smith railed against the power of mercantilist government officials in England who unfairly transferred wealth to themselves or their small group of friends, actions that perversely prevented the creation of wealth by the multitude of people through the free exchange of goods within and between countries. We see these same moral sentiments today in populist complaints about crony capitalism where government, in the name of picking winners and losers, is actually picking friends and enemies.

America's founders stressed these same principles of markets, incentives, and limited government. In the Declaration of Independence, they denounced the authoritarian monarchy "for cutting off our trade with all parts of the world" and "for imposing taxes on us without our consent." They clearly had incentives in mind when they put clause 8 into Article I, Section 8, of the Constitution: "To promote the Progress of Science and useful Arts, by securing for limited Times to Authors and Inventors the exclusive Right to their respective Writings and Discoveries."

Of course, they recognized the role of government "instituted among men" to secure the rights of "life, liberty and the pursuit of happiness," as Thomas Jefferson memorably put it. They relied on many checks and balances to limit the power of government officials, and in the Tenth Amendment they explicitly limited centralized power: "The powers not delegated to the United States by the Constitution, nor prohibited by it to the States, are reserved to the States respectively, or to the people."

The Special Importance of Predictability
and the Rule of Law

The two principles I put at the top of the list—policy predictability and the rule of law—are sometimes given less emphasis than markets, incentives, and limited government. Yet they are just as important. Indeed they have grown in importance.

Seventy years ago Friedrich Hayek wrote, in *The Road to Serfdom*, that "nothing distinguishes more clearly conditions in a free country from those in a country under arbitrary government than the observance in the former of the great principles known as the Rule of Law. Stripped of all technicalities, this means that government in all its actions is bound by rules fixed and announced beforehand—rules which make it possible to foresee with fair certainty how the authority will use its coercive powers in given circumstances and to plan one's individual affairs on the basis of this knowledge . . . [T]he discretion left to the executive organs wielding coercive power should be reduced as much as possible." Similarly in his 1962 classic *Capitalism and Freedom*, Milton Friedman argued for economic policies based on "a government of law instead of men," explaining its commonality with the arguments for "the first amendment to the Constitution and, equally, to the entire Bill of Rights."

In the time since Hayek and Friedman wrote their books, we have learned much more about the advantages of rules and predictability, especially in the modern world of high technology and fast-moving news and markets. If people are forward-looking and adjust their behavior to new circumstances, then economic policy works best when formulated as a rule. Government's adherence to known rules allows people to have a clearer sense of what is coming, and therefore to make more informed decisions about long-range plans.

Setting out a sensible rule and sticking to it also helps policymakers resist interest-group pressure. Rather than having to consider the merits of every special-interest plea for more government support, a rule can set a standard that applies to all cases and limits the role of government broadly. Rules can also avoid overreactions to short-term blips in the economy. They allow people to exercise their freedom and their judgment, and enable their leaders to keep their eyes on long-term goals.

Economists Finn Kydland and Edward Prescott won the Nobel Prize for showing that discretionary policies produce poor results by denying people the benefits of policy commitments. Such government commitments are needed for the proper functioning of a market economy. A commitment to a reasonably sound rule—even if it is very far from a perfect rule—is thus preferable to discretionary policies. Highly discretionary policy creates uncertainty and limits the ability of market participants to plan. It also tends to distort market behavior, driving it toward inefficient short-term responses.

Economist Robert Lucas, who was also awarded a Nobel Prize, developed a subtle yet key argument for predictability of policy and for the rule of law. He showed that clear policy rules are needed to determine how an economic policy would work. Since people's expectations are heavily dependent on future policy, effective evaluation of the policy requires stipulating not only what the policy will be today but also what it will be in the future. A policy rule or law does just that. In contrast, the evaluation of discretionary policies breaks down because people do not know what they imply for the future.

Defining Principles in Practice

No bright line can determine whether or not a particular policy satisfies the principles of economic freedom. The degree to which the principles are applied in practice depends on how they are interpreted and on how they are perceived to work in practice. Their application to particular issues depends on the commitment and motivation of government officials and on both internal and external constraints. And some policies may look good according to one criterion but look terrible according to the others, and would thereby fail miserably to satisfy the principles. Prohibition was made a rule of law by the Eighteenth Amendment to the Constitution, but its restrictions on buying and selling alcohol, unpredictable enforcement, and intrusion of government proved to be a disaster for the country.

When policymakers lean in the direction of economic freedom, they pursue less interventionist, more predictable, and more systematic policies. In the area of fiscal policy, legislators and executive-branch officials set long-term policies for spending and revenues consistent with a balanced budget; they rely on the automatic responses of tax revenues to fall in recessions and transfer payments to rise in recessions through programs built into the law—the so-called built-in stabilizers or automatic stabilizers—to help prevent and moderate booms or busts in a predictable way; they try to avoid short-term Keynesian discretionary interventions. In monetary policy, central-bank officials adhere to steady-as-you-go policies and rules for setting the amount of money in circulation and adjusting the interest rate to maintain the purchasing power of the currency.

In regulatory policy, government officials set clear rules based on what works and what doesn't, and regulators enforce those rules rather than use their power to deviate from them to help certain well-connected people or businesses. In safety-net and education programs, they tend to devolve decisions to state and local governments, where costs and benefits can be better assessed with on-the-ground knowledge. They worry about providing the right incentives to work or to save. More generally, when economic freedom is a guiding principle, the role of government is limited to areas where the market cannot do the job alone, such as national defense and justice, and is assigned when appropriate to state and local governments.

In contrast, when policymakers neglect economic freedom, they pursue less systematic, more interventionist policies; rather than long-lasting reform, they use temporary discretionary actions, which make it nearly impossible "to foresee with fair certainty," à la Hayek, future policy actions. Fiscal policy focuses on temporary and targeted stimulus programs, the goals of which are usually to produce a short-term gain with less concern about long-term sustainability. Monetary policy seeks to influence or respond to momentary economic fluctuations without a long-term strategy. Public policies to educate and assist people in need tend to be drawn into more powerful central government bureaucracies and away from towns and communities, where people know more and have more ability to vote with their feet.

Proving Grounds

Compared to most countries, and certainly compared to the broad sweep of human history, the United States has ranked high on the scales of economic and political freedom, with the principles being followed and applied much more often than not. That is why the country has generally been so prosperous and why millions immigrated from abroad to reap the economic rewards of hard work, ingenuity, and willingness to take risks.

But when we examine the history of American economic policy carefully, we see major movements between more and less economic freedom, more and less emphasis on rules-based policy, more and less expansive roles for government, more and less reliance on markets and incentives. The threshold for passing "the principles of economic freedom test" seems to have been raised and lowered over time.

We can see these movements very clearly in the past half century. A big move toward more interventionist policies occurred in the late 1960s and 1970s. This was followed by a shift toward more predictable policies and a more limited role for government in the 1980s and 1990s. More recently—and in my view this is the heart of our current predicament—we have seen a return toward more government intervention. Remarkably the movements occur nearly simultaneously for fiscal policy, monetary policy, regulatory policy, and tax policy. Each of these swings has had enormous consequences for the American economy. Taken together, they make for a historical proving ground to determine which policy direction is better for restoring America's prosperity. So let's review the facts.

Slipping toward Interventionism

Interventionist approaches to government policy became increasingly popular in American academia in the decades following World War II. In the sphere of macroeconomics this interventionism was commonly called Keynesian economics because it derived from the economic policy ideas put forth by John Maynard Keynes during the Great Depression of the 1930s. The emphasis was squarely on government activism.

Soon these ideas started to be expressed in actual policies, first in the Kennedy and Johnson administrations, and then continuing in the Nixon, Ford, and Carter administrations. They often took the form of temporary Keynesian countercyclical fiscal packages intended to drive aggregate demand or otherwise manipulate the economy. These included an investment tax credit in

1962 to stimulate the economy, a tax surcharge in 1968 to slow down the economy, a tax rebate in 1975 to stimulate the economy, a jobs tax credit in 1977 to stimulate jobs, and the public works programs with sizable grants to the states for infrastructure in 1977 and 1978.

In the 1960s the federal government began to interfere with private-sector wage and price decisions by giving firms and labor unions guidelines for such decisions. The epitome of the departure from the principles of economic freedom was the imposition of a wage and price freeze by the Nixon administration, the seeds of which were sown in the wage and price guidelines of the 1960s. Intended to combat inflation, the rate of which was creeping up owing to an overly expansionary monetary policy, the Nixon administration removed the decision of what price or wage to set from individuals and businesses and put it in the hands of government. The original ninety-day freeze on wages and prices, announced on August 15, 1971, expanded into a massive three-year experiment in discretionary government controls—an experiment that ultimately failed in its intended purpose of controlling inflation and caused a host of unintended consequences until the remnant of the controls on energy prices was finally removed a decade later.

The Federal Reserve applied the same interventionist approach to monetary policy. The 1960s and 1970s saw a series of discretionary adjustments of the growth in the supply of money, leading to booms and busts and ever-higher inflation. The Federal Reserve did not heed the advice of economists such as Milton Friedman, who, in a famous presidential address given before the American Economic Association in 1968, recommended one of the key principles of economic freedom, that the Federal Reserve go about "setting itself a steady course and sticking to it."

The Fed's actions were highly unstable and unpredictable over this period. First the Fed would ease up on monetary policy, raising money growth too much, and then inflation would pick up. Then it would tighten monetary policy, reducing the growth rate of the money supply, and a recession would result. The Fed would then fail to sustain the tighter policy long enough to yield a lasting decline in inflation. Again and again, short-term thinking led to uneven and irregular monetary decisions.

Back toward Economic Freedom

This interventionist approach began to wane as the 1970s drew to a close. Empirical studies on the effects of discretionary fiscal stimulus packages showed that they were not working as intended to stimulate the economy. Both inflation and unemployment were higher than they were before the interventionist approach. Americans were getting sick of the poorly performing economy. The incoming Reagan administration eschewed highly discretionary approaches. It favored a greater reliance on long-term reforms rather than temporary Keynesian stimulus packages.

Throughout the 1980s and 1990s, economic policy was decidedly noninterventionist, especially in comparison with policies like the damaging wage and price controls of the 1970s. More attention was paid to the principles of economic liberty. Monetary policy focused on price stability. Tax reform led to lower marginal tax rates. Regulatory reform encouraged competition and innovation. Welfare reform devolved decisions to the states. And with strong economic growth and spending restraint, the federal budget moved into balance by the end of the 1990s.

Fiscal policy that relied more on the automatic stabilizers, rather than discretionary policies, in responding to the ups and downs of the business cycle continued through the 1990s, with very few—and very modest—exceptions. President George H. W. Bush proposed a very small economic stimulus in 1992, but this failed to pass Congress. President Bill Clinton proposed another small stimulus in 1993, but it too failed to pass. By 1997, Northwestern University economist Martin Eichenbaum could write, with little opposition, of the "widespread agreement that countercyclical discretionary fiscal policy is neither desirable nor politically feasible."

The shift in monetary policy began quite abruptly with the Federal Reserve's decision—under the leadership of the new Federal Reserve chairman, Paul Volcker—to start focusing on inflation. This marked a dramatic change from most of the 1970s, when the Fed repeatedly switched emphasis from unemployment to inflation and back again. By 1983, in an address before the American Economic Association, Volcker was able to note with a sense of accomplishment that the Fed had "gone a long way toward changing the trends of the past decade and more." His successor, Alan Greenspan, maintained this commitment to price stability through the 1980s and 1990s.

The Fed also showed a greater appreciation for the importance of predictability and transparency in its decisions. In the 1970s, decisions about interest rates were hidden within the Fed's announcements about the growth of the supply of money. By the early 1990s, however, the Fed was announcing its interest-rate decisions immediately after making them—even publicly explaining its expectations and intentions for the future. And the transcripts of meetings of the Federal Open Market Committee—the Federal Reserve body that makes decisions about interest rates and the growth rate of money—include numerous references to policy rules as guidelines for policy in the 1990s. The empirical evidence assembled by Federal Reserve officials such as William Poole, president of the Federal Reserve Bank of St. Louis, and John Judd and Bharat Trehan, economists at the Federal Reserve Bank of St. Louis, plainly demonstrates that monetary policy corresponded far more closely to simple policy rules in the 1980s and 1990s than it had in the previous two decades.

Policy Veers Away Again

As the twenty-first century began, many hoped that applying these same limited-government and market-based policy principles to Social Security, education, and health care would create greater opportunities and better lives for all Americans. But policy veered in a different direction.

Public officials from both parties apparently found the limited-government approach to be a disadvantage, some simply because they wanted to do more—whether it was to tame the business cycle, increase homeownership, or provide the elderly with better drug coverage. They began to take the good economic performance for granted, forgetting that good economic policies made that performance possible. They forgot the earlier lessons that interventionist policies frequently made things worse; some even engaged in revisionist history, claiming that such policies could be counted on to have positive economic effects. Complacent about the success, they let down their guard against the ever-present political pressures that thwart good policy and lead to reckless ones. And so policy moved back in a more interventionist direction, with the federal government assuming greater powers.

The change in policy direction did not occur overnight. We saw increased federal intervention in the housing market beginning in the late 1990s. Perhaps an early warning sign of the change was the decision by the George W. Bush administration to respond to the economic downturn it confronted in 2001 with a onetime "tax rebate," in which $300 checks were sent to about two-thirds of American taxpayers, intended to stimulate demand. Though one could say it was the first installment on the more permanent 2001 tax cuts, that decision led Milton Friedman to pronounce with regret that "Keynesianism has risen from the dead," and especially given what has happened since then, he was certainly right.

Clear signs of activism can be found in monetary policy. Between 2003 and 2005, the Federal Reserve held interest rates far below the levels that would have been suggested by monetary policy rules that had guided the Fed's actions in the previous two decades. The deviation was large—on the order of magnitude seen in the unstable decade of the 1970s. The Fed's public statements during that time—which asserted that interest rates would be low for a "prolonged period" and would rise at a "measured pace"—are evidence that this was an intentional departure from the policies of the 1980s and 1990s.

That departure was intended to help ward off a perceived risk of deflation, but the extremely low interest rates during these years contributed to the development of the housing bubble that played the central role in the financial crisis that first flared up in 2007 and turned into a full-fledged panic in the fall of 2008. In February 2008 President Bush signed into law a $152 billion temporary stimulus package that again included checks to taxpayers. And, of course, interventionism reached a new peak with the massive government bailouts of Wall Street in 2008. The Fed began in March 2008 what would become a series of on-again/off-again bailouts of the creditors of Wall Street financial firms—on for the creditors of Bear Stearns, off for the creditors of Lehman Brothers, on for the creditors of AIG, and then off again while the Troubled Asset Relief Program (TARP) was rolled out. The original intent of the Bear Stearns intervention was to prevent the failure of that firm from spilling over and adversely affecting other firms and markets. But that bailout was not followed by a statement of a clear strategy of what would come next; instead the policy was quite unpredictable. Many expected that the creditors of Lehman Brothers would be bailed out too, if that firm failed, but when at the last minute the government suggested bankruptcy instead, the markets were shocked. The panic took on steam when the TARP was rolled out a week later. It was only then that the markets fell like a rock.

During the ensuing panic, the government took actions to assist the commercial-paper market and money-market mutual funds, and gave clear reasons and a strategy for doing so, which was an improvement over the other interventions. But then the bailouts were extended to automakers in Detroit, and the rule of law was twisted in yet another way: creditors whose claims had priorities were forced to step back in line and wait for others to be paid.

Following the panic, the government could have returned to the less interventionist policies that had worked in earlier decades. Indeed, during testimony in the U.S. Senate in November 2008 I strongly recommended such policies—long-lasting rather than temporary tax reductions for people with lower incomes, as well as a pledge to stop, or at least postpone for a substantial period, the tax rate increases that were scheduled to occur in the near future. Instead Washington doubled down on its interventionist policies. On the fiscal side, we saw extraordinary interventions—from the large $862 billion fiscal stimulus, which included temporary rebates and credits, as well as grants to state and local governments, to a slew of targeted programs including cash-for-clunkers and tax credits for first-time home buyers. On the monetary side, the Fed engaged in a super-loose monetary policy, including its massive quantitative-easing policy in 2009—now known as "QE1," which included the purchase of $1.25 trillion in mortgage-backed securities and $300 billion in long-term Treasury bonds—and again in 2010—now known as "QE2," which involved the purchase of another $600 billion in long-term Treasury bonds.

And the interventions did not stop with monetary and fiscal policy. Since 2009 we've added on complex regulatory interventions in health care (the Patient Protection and Affordable Care Act of 2010) and finance (the Dodd-Frank Wall Street Reform and Consumer Protection Act of 2010). An index of economic freedom prepared by the *Wall Street Journal* and the Heritage Foundation showed a record decline in 2010 and another decline in 2011. All told, there can be little doubt that the threshold for passing "the principles of economic freedom test" had been lowered substantially in the United States.

Look at the Evidence

What effect did these widely varying applications of principles of economic freedom have on the economy? The evidence is clear. The first move, toward less economic freedom, aligned with a period of frequent recessions, high unemployment, high inflation, and low growth from the late 1960s to the early 1980s. Inflation, unemployment, and interest rates all reached into double digits in this period, and by the late 1970s there was a palpable sense in America—not unlike today—that our economy was out of control and perhaps headed for an enduring decline. Indeed, productivity growth—the fundamental reason for rising living standards—slowed markedly in this period.

The second swing, toward more economic freedom, coincided with a remarkably stable period, frequently called the Great Moderation, from the mid-1980s until the early to mid-2000s. Unemployment declined dramatically. Job growth was amazingly strong—44 million jobs were created during the expansions of that period. Both the levels and the volatility of inflation and interest rates were markedly lower than they had been in the 1970s. The volatility of real GDP was reduced by half. Economic expansions were longer and stronger, while recessions were shorter and shallower than they had been in the previous two decades. It was a more stable and sustained-growth period than ever before in American history. By the mid-1990s, productivity growth began to pick up, reversing the productivity slowdown that started in the

1970s. Productivity growth had fallen from 2.6 percent in 1948–1969 to 1.6 percent in 1970–1995 but reestablished a 2.5 percent trend in 1996. America was on the road to prosperity again.

Finally, the swing back toward interventionism in recent years did not result in the intended improvement, but rather an epidemic of unintended consequences—a financial crisis and a recession much deeper than any of those during the Great Moderation period. Unemployment rose again, reversing the generally falling trend of the Great Moderation. Most disappointing of all was a recovery so anemic that it doesn't deserve to be called a recovery. Reflecting the doubling down of interventions since the recovery began, it is the worst economic recovery in American history. The new health care and financial laws are already raising costs and deterring new investment and risk-taking. Big government has proved to be a clumsy manager. This anemic recovery could have been avoided had the government returned to the principles of economic freedom.

Historical Timelines: Seeing Is Believing

We can visualize the evidence and learn more about the timing of the policy actions and their effects by looking at a timeline. The following chart shows the unem-

Timelines of Interventionism and Unemployment

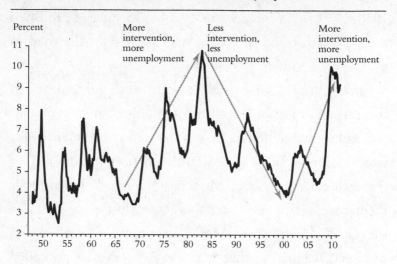

ployment rate—the percentage of people in the labor force who are unemployed—over time. To be counted as unemployed, one has to be looking for work. A person who stops looking for work and drops out of the labor market is not counted as unemployed. Thus the official unemployment rate shown here understates the degree of unemployment. Even so, the unemployment rate is quite high and is one of the most worrisome economic statistics in the United States.

The chart shows the unemployment rate from late 1946 through 2011. Unemployment goes up during recessions and down during recoveries. In the chart we can see frequent ups and downs; these are the recessions and recoveries. But in addition to these shorter-term ups and downs, we can also see bigger longer-term swings in unemployment.

I've split the chart into periods of time based on how interventionist policy was during each period, or on how much policy deviated from the principles of economic freedom, as defined earlier. The upward-sloping lines correspond to times when policy was more interventionist. The downward-sloping line corresponds to the time of less interventionism. Of course, the dates cannot be determined precisely, but in each case the date is near the time when talk about policy change began.

Observe that during the more interventionist periods, unemployment moved upward, and that during the less interventionist periods, unemployment moved back down. In the late 1960s and 1970s, unemployment rose higher step-by-step in each recession, with the top and bottom of each step higher than the previous one. From 4.0 percent in 1965, the unemployment rate reached 6.1 percent in 1971, 9.0 percent in 1975, and 10.8 percent in 1982. Inflation, not shown in this chart, also rose. From 2 percent in 1965, inflation reached 6 percent in 1970, 12 percent in 1974, and 15 percent in 1980.

Then in the 1980s and 1990s, unemployment reversed course in several steps, with each step lower than the previous one. From a peak of 10.8 percent in 1982 the unemployment rate fell to 5.2 percent in 1989 and 4.0 percent in 2000.

More recently, following the period I classify as interventionist, the unemployment rate has moved up again, reaching 10.1 percent in 2009, and then has hardly come down at all through 2010 into 2011.

What Came First?

While the facts in the chart are indisputable, some may doubt the interpretation that changes in adherence to the policy principles caused economic performance to change. An alternative view is that poor economic performance brought about more interventionism, or perhaps that good economic performance permitted policymakers to focus more on the principles of economic freedom. The simple timing of events, however, disproves such a view.

The interventionist fiscal policies that began in the 1960s obviously could not have been a response to the deep recessions and high inflation of the 1970s. Similarly, the discretionary monetary policy that began in the 1960s could not have been caused by the inflation of the 1970s. And it obviously strains credibility to argue that the less interventionist move in the early 1980s was caused by the low inflation and stable economy of the 1980s and 1990s.

Perhaps more plausibly, some might argue that the shift

back to interventionism in recent years was provoked by the severe financial panic in the fall of 2008, which turned a mild recession into a very deep recession. But interventionism began before the panic of the fall of 2008: low interest rates were maintained from 2003 through 2005; the Bush administration's stimulus packages were enacted in June 2001 and February 2008; the Fed's discretionary bailouts began in March 2008. Moreover, if the emergency of the panic was the reason for the move toward discretionary policies, one would have expected to see a return to more rules-based policies once the height of that panic passed. Instead, the Fed undertook another large discretionary action—QE2—and rationalized it on the quintessentially discretionary grounds that the economic recovery was too slow.

The more straightforward conclusion—that implementing the principles of economic freedom was an important cause of the improved performance of the 1980s and 1990s, and that deviation from those principles has been harmful to the economy—aligns much better with the historical timeline.

Are There Smoking Guns?

There is plenty of corroborating evidence about specific interventions that bolsters the findings from the broad movements in economic freedom. Princeton economist Alan Blinder studied temporary tax changes—including the 1975 rebate—and found that they had a much smaller and uncertain effect than permanent changes. He also studied the 1971–1974 wage and price controls, and found that they had at best a temporary effect on inflation and that their dismantling caused a "burst of 'double digit' inflation." Many studies have shown that the boom-bust monetary policy caused the boom-bust economic performance and the high inflation of the 1970s.

My own research showed that the low interest rates set by the Fed in 2003–2005 accelerated the housing-price boom, and thus led to the large housing bust. It also led to risk-taking as investors and financial institutions searched for higher yields. The research also revealed that a more rules-based federal funds rate would have prevented much of the housing boom and bust. Other economists have found much the same. Economist George Kahn of the Federal Reserve Bank of Kansas City showed that were it not for the Fed's deviation from the principles it followed in the 1980s and 1990s, the housing bubble would have been significantly less severe. Without those deviations, he concluded that "the bubble in housing prices looks more like a bump."

I found that the tax rebates and onetime payments in 2001, 2008, and 2009 did little in the aggregate to jump-start consumption and thereby jump-start the economy. This finding is consistent with the so-called permanent income theory, which predicts that most consumers consider their income over longer periods of time before adjusting their consumption. In another study, John Cogan and I found that the parts of the 2009 stimulus aimed at boosting government purchases were ineffective. In my view, QE1 had at most a small effect on mortgage rates once prepayment risk and default risk were controlled for.

Moreover, the highly discretionary on-again/off-again bailout policies of the Fed did not prevent the panic that began in September 2008; in my view they were a likely cause of the panic, or at least made the panic worse. The unpredictable nature of these interventions could have been avoided if the Fed and the Treasury had stated more clearly the reasons behind the Bear Stearns intervention and their intentions for future policy. But no such description was provided. Confusion about policy rose when the TARP was rolled out, and panic ensued as the S&P 500 fell by 30 percent. The original stated purpose of the TARP—to buy up low-quality assets on banks' balance sheets—was never credibly viewed as operational, and it caused uncertainty. It was only when the purpose of the TARP was changed—to inject equity into the banks— and clarified on October 13, 2008, that the panic subsided.

To be sure, the Fed's interventions into the commercial-paper market and the money-market funds were helpful in rebuilding confidence. So not every discretionary intervention was harmful, but these would not have been necessary had the earlier interventions been avoided.

There are other damaging effects of the discretionary actions. The fiscal packages have increased the national debt, which raises uncertainty about how it will be paid off. The monetary interventions have reduced central-bank independence, because many of them are not monetary policy as conventionally defined, but rather fiscal policy or credit allocation policy. And there is a risk of inflation if they are not unwound.

What About the 1930s?

I have focused in this chapter on relatively recent U.S. history because I think it is most relevant for the problem America faces. But policymakers and commentators frequently look to the experience of the Great Depression for guidance, and no self-respecting policymaker should ignore the 1930s.

In my view the history lessons from the 1930s are much the same as those from more recent years. Like the 1970s and our more recent economic woes, the Great Depression was caused by a series of harmful government actions and

interventions that cut across both political parties. This is
the implication of the now-classic historical research in
Milton Friedman and Anna Schwartz's *Monetary History of
the United States*, Allan Meltzer's more recent *History of the
Federal Reserve*, and Amity Shlaes's even more recent *The
Forgotten Man*. The actions and interventions began in the
Hoover administration and were doubled down in the
Franklin D. Roosevelt administration. That's why unemployment was still 15 percent in 1940, compared to the 5
percent it was ten years earlier when the economy started
contracting, and why the Dow Jones Industrial Average
was still less than half the value it was in October 1929.

Though sometimes described otherwise, Herbert
Hoover was much more an interventionist than his pre-
decessor and fellow Republican Calvin Coolidge. Amity
Shlaes shows how Hoover "disdained laissez-faire economics as 'theoretic and emotional.' " His popularity was
based on his amazing hands-on interventions to assist
refugees in World War I and to provide aid after natural disasters in the United States, which, while improving
the lives of many people, demonstrated a bias toward government interventions.

As a result he ignored some of the basic principles of
economic freedom by signing the highly protection-
ist Smoot-Hawley Tariff Act in 1930, even though 1,028
economists signed a letter urging him not to. He also

First Principles

intervened with businesses in their decisions about prices and wages, which accentuated the downturn, and he watched while the Federal Reserve contracted the amount of money in circulation, thereby worsening the banking panic and the economic contraction. In 1932 he increased tax rates. The top marginal rate was raised from 25 percent to 63 percent.

Roosevelt then doubled down with one of the most interventionist government actions of all time in the United States, the National Industrial Recovery Act (NIRA), enacted into law in 1933. Under the law, American industries could establish standards or codes by which they could keep prices and wages high, choking off competition, and the President could tell individual firms not to cut prices or wages. Economists Harold Cole of the University of Pennsylvania and Lee Ohanian of UCLA found in their research that this and similar laws "violated the most basic economic principles by suppressing competition, and setting prices and wages in many sectors well above their normal levels." In 1936 a tax, which reached as high as 70 percent, was put on retained corporate earnings. To make matters worse, in 1937 the Federal Reserve increased the amount of deposits that banks were required to hold at the Fed, which pulled money out of circulation.

There is no evidence for the view that Keynesian countercyclical discretionary fiscal policy in the 1930s ended the Great Depression. After all, unemployment was still 15 percent in 1940, when the economy began to gear up for the extraordinary sacrifices of the war effort in the 1940s. After the war ended, the U.S. economy started growing rapidly again in the 1950s without the drag of the NIRA, without more tax rate increases, and with a more sensible fiscal and monetary policy.

The Way Forward

If neglect of the principles of economic freedom has caused the American economy to grow weak, then it's time to reapply those principles and get the economy moving again. Grab the proverbial policy pendulum, pull it back toward the principles of economic freedom, and make sure it never swings back again.

To do so, however, we have to understand what causes those pendulum swings. The harmful swing toward interventionist policies in the 1960s and 1970s was supported by Democrats and Republicans alike. So was the less interventionist swing in the 1980s and 1990s. So was the recent interventionist revival, and so can be the restoration of less interventionist policy going forward. But who were the decision-makers responsible for the mistakes and the successes? What lessons are to be learned? I address these questions in the next chapter.

2

. . . . .

Who Gets Us In and Out of These Messes?

W hy does adherence to the principles of economic freedom ebb and flow over time? Based on my experience working in government, advising politicians, talking with economists, I see two basic forces at work.

First is the strength of the underlying support for the principles. There are, of course, differences of opinion about the importance of economic freedom. Some see little reason to support it strongly, arguing that it gets in the way of other objectives, either their own or their perception of the country's objectives. When those opposition voices grow louder or more influential, support for the principles wanes.

Second is the ability or commitment of public officials who support the principles in theory to take on the difficult task of implementing them in practice. To get the job done, they not only have to be clear about the principles but also have to explain them, fight for them, and then decide when and how much to compromise on them. The challenge represents an age-old problem in the art of political economy.

Compromise and Malaise

My first job as an economist in Washington, D.C., was during a period when the winds of economic freedom were not blowing much at all.* It was the summer of 1976. I took a job as senior economist on President Gerald Ford's Council of Economic Advisers, moving to Wash-

---

* It was not my first stint in Washington. I worked as a naval officer in the Defense Department in the late 1960s, trying to use economic-like optimization models to help detect Soviet submarines. While no easy task, in retrospect I found applying optimization principles to defense policy rather straightforward compared to applying the principles of economics to the complexity of economic policymaking.

ington from New York City, where I had been teaching at Columbia University. I was still in my twenties, and for a young economist interested in policy, I thought this was the best job in America, perhaps in the world. Nothing like the Council—a small group of professional economists and statisticians in close proximity to the leader of the country—exists in other countries.

Alan Greenspan chaired the Council at the time. He valued the principles of economic freedom, and I was pleased and excited that he hired me. Greenspan had long been, and remains to this day, obsessed with economic facts and figures, always trying to find ways to test hunches about the economy. This focus was fine with me because I was similarly obsessed. We used to joke back and forth about who had a better "nose for numbers," who could better spot a trend or an anomaly in a column of figures. Greenspan had also developed some other useful but entirely different skills: he was a close confidant of President Ford, which meant that the economists who worked with him had a good chance of having their views heard and even acted on by the President.

The economy was in between two boom-bust cycles in 1976, still recovering from the 1973–1975 recession but well before the 1980 recession. Unfortunately for President Ford, the economic recovery slowed down that summer, and he lost the 1976 election to Jimmy Carter.

Economic growth dropped from a very high 9 percent in the first quarter of 1976 to only 2 percent in the third quarter; unemployment rose, and this was enough to swing the election to Carter. I stayed on to work on President Carter's Council of Economic Advisers—Charles Schultze of the Brookings Institution took over from Greenspan as chairman—before returning to New York the following year to teach and do research at Columbia and to work with Greenspan at his Wall Street consulting firm.

One of my jobs on President Ford's Council was drafting sections of the *Economic Report of the President*, a legally mandated responsibility of the Council. For that year's *Report*, we aimed to lay out some principles of fiscal policy based on recent experience and to warn about the costs of deviating from those principles. We thought this would be a useful contribution whether or not Ford won the election. Not surprisingly, given Greenspan's views, the principles were quite consistent with the principles of economic freedom outlined in chapter 1.

In fact, the *Report* was quite noninterventionist—anti-Keynesian would not be too strong a description. One of the principles—italicized for emphasis and placed at the top of a page—was *"Tax reduction should be permanent rather than in the form of a temporary rebate."* As a twenty-something newcomer to the presidential policy game, I loved finding ways to put good economic ideas into a major White House policy document, including the "permanent income theory," which I had learned in graduate school and had taught my students.

Ironically, however, a year earlier President Ford had done just what we were warning against in the *Report*. Responding to the popular clamor to "do something" to stimulate the economy, he proposed in his 1975 State of the Union speech a temporary one-year tax cut. Congress then added a onetime increase in Social Security benefits and, to bolster the sagging housing market, a onetime tax credit for new home buyers. The result was the Tax Reduction Act of 1975, which was 40 percent larger than Ford had proposed. But he signed it into law anyway. So the *Report* was a pretty blatant case of do-as-I-say-not-as-I-do advice.

Indeed, we found that the 1975 tax rebate led to only a temporary blip in consumer spending, and by the time the rebates were finished, spending was declining from the blip and so was economic growth. Thus the economic growth slowdown from the very high growth earlier in the year was likely related to that rebate. Based on this empirical experience, we wrote in the 1976 *Economic Report of the President* that "temporary tax cuts are not consistent with the objective of sustaining economic expansion." We were drawing lessons from the 1975 rebate.

One could have argued a year ago that it was a mistake in principle, but now it was a mistake in practice. And the lessons were not only economic but also political: the quarterly up and down in economic growth in 1976 was at least partly caused by the rebate, and to the extent that the slowdown cost Ford the election, the rebate was bad politics as well as bad economics.

But I cannot say that Greenspan or the Council of Economic Advisers advised against the 1975 tax rebate when it was under consideration, or that they fought against it and lost. Signing that bill was a close call for President Ford right up to the last minute. When the final bill from the House-Senate conference committee came to the White House with the other temporary measures included—the onetime additional Social Security payments and a home buyers credit—Ford asked that two messages be prepared, a veto message and a signing message, so that he could have more time to decide. He then asked for written opinions about whether to sign the bill. His Treasury Secretary, William Simon, recommended against it. But Greenspan advised signing it, writing a one-sentence memo: "I recommend that the tax bill be signed, but that you simultaneously come down very hard on expenditure increases." In the end, the President signed the bill.

There went the principles. The 1975 decision represented a compromise in which some principles were sacrificed in exchange for others, such as holding down the growth of spending as Greenspan recommended in his memo. Despite his own misgivings about such interventions, Greenspan compromised, thinking that no bill (or a worse bill) would be more harmful to the economy than the bill with the rebate. Moreover, with both the House and the Senate controlled by the opposition party, the veto would likely be overridden anyway. So better for the economy and the President to show that Washington politicians were working together.

Continued support for interventionist policies in much of the economics profession also explains Greenspan's compromise. While Greenspan himself was skeptical of fine-tuning, it was easier to give in on an issue that many economists still favored. In fact, moving in an anti-Keynesian direction would have been going against the tide of opinion in the economics profession. Keynesian ideas about countercyclical fiscal policy were still popular after first entering the debate in Washington in the early 1960s. At the time the 1975 bill was signed into law, the empirical evidence that discretionary Keynesian policies did not work was still accumulating and obviously did not include the disappointing experience with the 1975 rebate itself.

This contrasts with economic policymaking in the Carter administration. The election of 1976 brought into government a group of economists firmly in the Keynesian interventionist camp, including Charlie Schultze, who would lead the Council. Schultze had earlier served as budget director under Lyndon Johnson. He was a dedicated public servant with the best of intentions. He was gregarious, down to earth, and hard not to like. But he was not interested in the advice on less intervention and the warnings from the last *Economic Report of the President* written by Ford's Council. Indeed, after my involvement in that *Report*, Charlie reassigned me to another job. I was taken off the countercyclical fiscal policy beat and assigned to a back-burner project on tax reform. The new administration then doubled down on interventionist fiscal policy, with President Carter signing more stimulus bills into law in 1977. It was not a matter of compromising on the principles of economic freedom, as with Ford and Greenspan. It was a matter of outright objection to the principles, believing that there were better ways to restore a strong and prosperous economy.

The Carter stimulus packages included a temporary tax credit for firms hiring new workers as well as an infrastructure program, which sent federal public works grants to the states to build roads and bridges. Charlie Schultze explained that the packages were "designed to tread prudently between the twin risks of over and understimulation." But the stimulus packages did not work well. Later, President Carter's own deputy assistant Secretary of the Treasury for tax policy, Emil Sunley, found that "the impact of the credit on jobs was slight." Economist Edward "Ned" Gramlich, who years later would be appointed by President Clinton to the Federal Reserve Board, found that the public works grants did not stimulate infrastructure building by the states, which led him to conclude that "the general idea of stimulating the economy through state and local governments is probably not a very good one."

Economic performance during the Carter administration turned out to be terrible, plagued by rising unemployment and rising inflation. The press widely used the term "malaise" to describe President Carter's assessment of the country at this time. And this malaise was the main reason why Carter served a single term. He was swept out of Washington along with the interventionist policies that had led to the terrible performance. It was during this time that the climate of opinion began to change rapidly, and we could hear the ideas of economic freedom stirring again.

Before we can understand what happened next, we need to go back a little further in time and examine how interventionist policies, so evident in the Ford and Carter administrations, initially were applied in the Kennedy and Johnson administrations, with strong ideological support from within, and then strangely continued in the Nixon administration even without that support.

When the Keynesian Activists Came to Town

The Keynesian movement in America began in academia, and in particular in Cambridge, Massachusetts, led by Alvin Hansen at Harvard University and Paul Samuelson at MIT. Hansen's seminar at Harvard and his popular book, *A Guide to Keynes*, were largely responsible for bringing the ideas of John Maynard Keynes from Britain to the United States. Samuelson, who learned from Hansen as a student at Harvard before he moved to MIT, brought Keynesian ideas to virtually every student of economics in America in the 1950s and 1960s through his well-written and popular textbook *Economics*. Samuelson was also a brilliant mathematical economist who would transform the Department of Economics at MIT from a backwater into one of the best economics departments in the country, a position it still holds today. Along with Harvard, Samuelson's department was the place to go to learn Keynesian economics and the interventionist approach to policy. Legions of students who would go on to influential careers in government and academia were trained in Keynesian economics in the department that Samuelson created.

Paul Samuelson was the principle economic adviser to John F. Kennedy during the 1960 election campaign. After Kennedy won the election, Samuelson, as he later explained, "recruited the team for his Council of Economic Advisers," people like Walter Heller, who became the chair, and James Tobin, who became a member, both respected scholars of Keynesian economics and highly articulate spokesmen. Though Tobin served on the Council for only one year, his influence on the economics profession and on policy lasted for many years after he returned to teaching at Yale University.

The essence of the Keynesian approach to economic policy is the use, by government officials, of discretionary actions and interventions to prevent or mitigate recessions or to speed up recoveries. To be clear, this does not mean that certain distinctive features of Keynes's model of the economy—such as the existence of sticky prices, which cause some markets to adjust slowly, or the lack of aggregate demand as a reason for economic downturns—are wrong. In my own research these complex dynamic adjustments are a reason for policymakers to use more predictable rule-like policies, the polar opposite of Keynesian activism.

The Keynesian approach to policy activism received its official imprimatur in Washington politics and policy when Heller, Tobin, and their colleagues wrote the first *Economic Report of the President* for the Kennedy administration, published in 1962. The *Report* made an explicit case for significant discretion and intervention in economic policy. "The task of economic stabilization cannot be left entirely to built-in stabilizers," the *Report* warned. "Discretionary budget policy, e.g. changes in tax rates or expenditure programs, is indispensable—sometimes to reinforce, sometimes to offset, the effects of the stabilizers."

The Council further argued in the *Report* that the government should have broad leeway to make such changes in response to evolving conditions: "In order to promote economic stability, the government should be able to change quickly tax rates or expenditure programs, and equally able to reverse its actions as circumstances change." According to the Council, a similar approach should prevail in monetary policy—where "discretionary policy is essential, sometimes to reinforce, sometimes to mitigate or overcome, the monetary consequences of short-run fluctuations of economic activity."

This influential *Report* also made the case for wage and price "guideposts," which indicated to firms and workers just how much to limit their price or wage increases in the hope of keeping the inflation rate down as monetary and fiscal policy increased demand. The guideposts

expanded the role of government in the economy by trying to influence directly the decisions of the private firms,
their customers, and employees.

The Competing View

In 1962, the same year of the first *Report* from the Kennedy administration, University of Chicago economist
Milton Friedman published his book *Capitalism and Freedom*, which made the case for an entirely different position
about the role of government in the economy. Indeed, the
opening salvo of that book strongly criticized the more
expansive and interventionist role of government that
Kennedy argued for in his inaugural address of 1961.

There were two competing views: the Samuelson view
emanating from Cambridge and the Friedman view emanating from Chicago. The fundamental disagreement was
not over which instrument of government policy worked
better—monetary policy or fiscal policy—though there
was plenty of well-publicized debate about that. Rather the
real disagreement concerned the principles of economic
freedom. The economic freedom side argued that interventionist economic policies were not needed and were
actually harmful. They led to unpredictability, weakened
incentives, relied too little on the market, and expanded
the scope of government into areas where it was not justi-

fied. The Samuelson side argued that extensive intervention was essential to the stability of a market economy.

In a debate with Heller in 1969, Friedman explained that "the available evidence . . . casts grave doubt on the possibility of producing any fine adjustments in economic activity by fine adjustments in monetary policy—at least in the present state of knowledge . . . There are thus serious limitations to the possibility of a discretionary monetary policy and much danger that such a policy may make matters worse rather than better . . . The basic difficulties and limitations of monetary policy apply with equal force to fiscal policy . . . Political pressures to 'do something' . . . are clearly very strong indeed in the existing state of public attitudes. The main moral to be had from these two preceding points is that yielding to these pressures may frequently do more harm than good. There is a saying that the best is often the enemy of the good, which seems highly relevant . . . The attempt to do more than we can will itself be a disturbance that may increase rather than reduce instability."

Friedman was a resolute champion of these views, making the case whenever and wherever he could. He was a vociferous debater, quick on his feet, and with facts on the tip of his tongue. At the same time, he was respectful, never failing to answer a letter (or e-mails many years later) and always avoiding personal attacks. I once asked him why he took the time to answer so many letters from strangers. He told me that if someone took the time to write to him with a question, he felt he should find the time to answer.

Activism Marches On

Despite the efforts of Friedman and others, the interventionist view was winning in practice in the 1960s. Samuelson and his protégés had the ear of those in power, and Friedman did not. In addition, at least in the early 1960s there was not a lot of evidence one way or the other about interventionist policies, and certainly not enough to prove, as skeptics worried, that they were ineffective. With strong backing for the policies from many in the economics profession, and with skilled people in government to implement them, the activist policy started coming fast and furious.

Aside from the important permanent reduction in income tax rates in the Kennedy-Johnson tax cuts of 1964, policy was of the temporary, targeted variety, such as the temporary investment tax credit, the wage and price guidelines, and soon monetary policy as well. Ironically, the good expansion that followed the permanent tax cuts of 1964—which reduced the top tax rate from 91 percent to 70 percent—may have made the much different temporary Keynesian interventions look good by association, and they remained popular, at least until economists had the time to study their individual effects.

Getting the Fed to Cooperate

William McChesney Martin was the Federal Reserve chairman from 1951 until 1970. In the early 1950s Martin was largely responsible for restoring the Fed's independence from the Treasury after World War II. This independence—granted in the Accord of 1951—freed Martin to keep inflation from rising, and he did just that in the 1950s. That type of policy ended in the mid-1960s, when Martin began to let the money supply rise more rapidly and tried to keep interest rates low, which put upward pressure on inflation. The inflation rate started rising around 1965, long before the oil price shock caused by the Arab oil embargo of 1973, a factor that some Keynesians blamed for the inflation.

Why did Martin succumb to the activist views and move monetary policy in this direction? Martin was always interested in working together with the administration in power, and he had a rather relaxed view about the Fed's independence. As Martin explained it, "I do not believe it is consistent to have an agent [the Fed] so independent that it can undertake, if it chooses, to defeat the financing of a large deficit, which is a policy of the Congress."

Martin was persuaded by the Kennedy and Johnson administrations' argument that monetary policy should be coordinated with the administration's fiscal policy. Early on, under strong pressure from the Kennedy administration and after initial resistance, he agreed to the so-called Operation Twist. Under this program, the Fed bought long-term Treasury bonds and sold short-term Treasury bills. The aim was to keep long-term interest rates low, in order to spur investment, and at the same time keep shorter-term interest rates relatively high so that international investors would not move their funds overseas and put downward pressure on the value of the dollar.

Coordinating monetary policy with a more interventionist fiscal policy obviously meant that monetary policy would become more discretionary. As monetary historian Allan Meltzer argues in his history of the Fed, "Coordination meant that the Federal Reserve would not raise interest rates much, if at all," even if that might risk higher inflation.

Martin had also been persuaded by a new theory put forth by administration economists: that there was a policy trade-off in which lower unemployment could be achieved with higher inflation. Paul Samuelson and his

MIT colleague Robert Solow endorsed this idea, and the Council of Economic Advisers promoted it in the 1960s. The trade-off concept lessened Martin's resolve to keep inflation from rising, because he was persuaded that higher inflation would reduce unemployment. Theory aside, the political pressure to cooperate was probably the more powerful reason for the move to an activist Fed: as we will see, even when the economic arguments were proved wrong, the inflationary policy continued.

The Nixon Shock

Surprisingly, interventionist fiscal and monetary policies continued after Richard Nixon won the presidential election in 1968. Judging from the generally noninterventionist free-market pronouncements of President Nixon and the leanings of many economists in his administration— George Shultz (Secretary of Labor, Budget Director, Secretary of Treasury), Arthur Burns (White House adviser and then Fed chairman), Paul McCracken (chairman of the Council of Economic Advisers), and outside adviser Milton Friedman—one would have expected a reversal of policy. Indeed, early on in the administration this appeared to be the case, as one can see from reading contemporary accounts or talking with the people involved in making the decisions during that period.

One of the best contemporary accounts is that of Milton Friedman, who was writing a regular column in *Newsweek* magazine at the time. In a column published in the July 26, 1971, edition, Friedman was full of praise for Nixon's economic policy. He referred in detail to an economic policy speech given earlier that year by George Shultz, "Prescription for Economic Policy: 'Steady as You Go.'" Shultz made the case for the steadier, longer-term, more predictable policy that the Nixon administration was beginning to follow, in contrast to the late 1960s policy it had inherited from President Johnson. By sticking to those principles, Shultz argued, inflation would come down, unemployment would come down, and the economy would grow nicely.

Friedman titled his column "Steady as You Go," giving due credit to Shultz, and explained that Nixon had begun to reverse the harmful interventionist policy of the Johnson administration, which Friedman called "fine-tuning with a sledge hammer!" He was looking forward to a more stable and prosperous decade. But that decade didn't come to pass, because Nixon soon gave up on "steady as you go" for political reasons before it could yield positive results. He shifted his economic policy in an interventionist direction, with deleterious economic results that continued for a decade. Had Nixon stayed the course, the 1970s would likely have been a decade of strong growth with low inflation and low unemployment, much as we eventually saw in the 1980s and 1990s.

The shift happened on August 15, 1971, in a Sunday-evening television speech to the nation: Nixon announced a freeze on wages and prices. The announcement was certainly a shock, but it paved the way for an even more shocking series of monetary and fiscal policy interventions. Thinking that the wage and price controls would keep inflation in check, the Fed aggressively increased the growth rate of the supply of money. But that higher growth rate of money put upward price pressure on the economy, eventually leading to double-digit inflation, double-digit interest rates, and double-digit unemployment.

The August 15 policy change and the events of the next few years were a surprise and disappointment for those who were looking for change and knew that a continuation of the interventionist policies would fail. Of course, Friedman soon withdrew all his praise. He opened his May 14, 1973, column with "In a masterpiece of bad timing, I chose in the *Newsweek* issue of July 26, 1971, to pen a tribute to President Nixon's 'vision and courage' in following a policy of (1) steady and moderate fiscal restraint, (2) steady and moderate monetary restraint, (3) and avoidance of price and wage controls—a policy which George Shultz had earlier termed 'steady as you go' . . . Within six months of my column, all three elements had been abandoned."

Friedman predicted that economic performance would be very poor following this change in policy. He was right. It was not until the interventionist approach was finally abandoned in the 1980s and 1990s that economic performance finally improved. Looking back on those events and that speech now, George Shultz says, "Unfortunately, I lost this battle when [Treasury Secretary] John Connally persuaded President Nixon to institute wage-and-price controls. They were initially popular but, in the end, they produced all the predictable problems with which we are all too familiar."

What caused Nixon to move in this direction? As is often the case, the principles of economic freedom were sacrificed for pure political gain. Nixon grew impatient with Shultz's "steady as you go" idea. It was taking too much time. He began listening to John Connally, the former Democratic Texas governor whom he had appointed to be Secretary of the Treasury. Connally was not particularly committed to the principles of economic freedom despite being Treasury Secretary. He seemed to brag about being unprincipled, saying, as Shultz recalls, that "I can sell it square or I can sell it round." Nixon was worried about the looming 1972 election, and as Shultz put it, "An economist's lag is a politician's nightmare."

Nixon's freeze was very popular at first. "People favored the actions by a more than 4 to 1 margin," Paul McCracken, chairman of the Council of Economic Advisers, recalled, "and for women the margin was 6 to 1." Only a few economists objected at the time the controls were imposed. But then, during the next three years, the controls were extended into a second phase and a third phase. Soon the consumer price index started rising again and went to double-digit rates as the economy headed into the 1973–1975 recession. By that time most economists were claiming they had been opposed to the controls all along!

In practice, the wage and price controls brought interventionism beyond what anyone could have imagined when they thought about the idea in principle. To administer the freeze, government bureaucrats had to consider the intricate details of production and product definition. At a meeting on August 17, 1971, in the Roosevelt Room in the West Wing of the White House, Nixon's advisers were debating such things as whether chicken broilers were a raw agricultural product and thereby exempt from the price freeze, or a processed product and thereby subject to the freeze. Paul McCracken soon quit as chairman of the Council. George Shultz went from the budget office to the Treasury and then resigned in May 1974. But the measure had the support of one very prominent economic official who did not resign. Federal Reserve

Chairman Arthur Burns, who had been known as a free-market economist and teacher of Milton Friedman before he moved to Washington, defended the Nixon administration's efforts. He argued that "wage rates and prices no longer respond as they once did to the play of market forces." Either Burns had completely abandoned his principles or he was compromising big time.

Nixon resigned on August 9, 1974, in the wake of the Watergate scandal, but the efforts to micromanage wages and prices continued under President Ford. He established a Council on Wage and Price Stability and then engaged in a strange campaign to reduce inflation. He called it "Whip Inflation Now," which included a "WIN" button that people could wear on their lapel. He decided to announce the plan in a big speech before a joint session of Congress in October 1974. His economic advisers, including Alan Greenspan, as well as his Chief of Staff, Donald Rumsfeld, were in strong disagreement. Greenspan felt the speech was risky and recommended that Ford cancel it. But Ford refused even to change the speech, telling Rumsfeld, "Don, I think it is a good program."

During the speech, Ford wore the WIN button. He said it was "the symbol of this new mobilization, which I am wearing on my lapel. It bears the single word WIN. I think that tells it all. I will call upon every American to join in this massive mobilization and stick with it until we do win as a nation and as a people." His idea was that firms and workers would not set higher prices nor ask for higher wages as part of a public service, even if it were not in their own interest. The new intervention effort went nowhere. Shortly thereafter, the depth of the 1974–1975 recession caused policymakers to intervene in other ways, including through tax rebates and other stimulus programs taken up by Ford and Carter for the reasons described in the opening of this chapter.

Of course, the WIN campaign could not possibly work while the Federal Reserve continued with its inflationary policy. Nixon appointed Burns to replace Martin as chairman of the Fed in 1970, so Martin had overlapped with the Nixon administration for a year after the 1968 election. Interestingly, one of the reasons for the inflationary policy in the 1960s—the trade-off suggesting that higher inflation would bring lower unemployment—was taken off the table by the economists coming in with Nixon. They knew that research had disproved that trade-off, and they brought these new findings to Washington. But Martin, and Burns after him, continued the inflationary policies anyway. The political pressures on them overruled the economic evidence. As Allan Meltzer put it, "The members of the Council of Economic Advisers in the Nixon administration brought different ideas but no less inflation . . . These analytic changes could have served as the basis for a successful anti-inflation policy, but they were not used for that purpose."

Back from the Brink

It's difficult to recall now the seriousness of the U.S. economic slump by the end of the 1970s. Economic growth was weakening, unemployment was rising, and the dollar was sinking. Confidence in U.S. economic leadership was plunging at home and abroad. Sound familiar?

But then the winds of economic freedom started blowing again, starting with very strong gusts at the start of the incoming Reagan administration. No more short-term actions and interventions. Temporary was out. Permanent was in. Reagan proposed and the Congress passed long-term reforms such as the tax rate reductions, which reduced income tax rates by 25 percent across the board.

Both strong support for the principles and unwavering commitment to implement them were responsible for this rapid change. Of course, Ronald Reagan himself was committed. He was a firm believer in the principles of economic freedom, an avid reader and follower of economists like Friedman and Hayek. Between the time he failed to unseat President Ford in the 1976 Republican primaries and his announcement to run again in 1980, Reagan gave innumerable radio addresses putting forth his principles. He used down-home stories of economic freedom that he could tell in three minutes or less. He did not use ghost-writers. He wrote these out in long hand on lined yellow paper as he traveled around the country, as Kiron Skinner, Annelise Anderson, and Martin Anderson later carefully documented in their book *Reagan in His Own Hand*. The failed policies of the 1970s made Reagan's case appealing across the political spectrum. He based his election campaign on these principles, and he won.

Reagan appointed to his administration a large number of economic officials who were firmly committed to implementing the principles. Whereas Paul Samuelson recruited like-minded economists to the Council of Economic Advisers in the 1960s, Milton Friedman had a similar role in the 1980s. No members of the original Council under Reagan had come from the Samuelson school of thought in Cambridge, Massachusetts, and most during the entire Reagan period were influenced by Friedman. Over at the Treasury, Reagan appointed Norman Ture, who had a Ph.D. in economics from the University of Chicago, as the Under Secretary to oversee tax policy. And he appointed Beryl Sprinkel, another economist with a Ph.D. from Chicago, as the Under Secretary to oversee monetary and financial issues. Both

Ture and Sprinkel were known for their single-minded and unwavering focus on permanently lower tax rates and less interventionism.

In addition, Reagan appointed a group of outside advisers, most of whom were economists committed to the principles of economic freedom, and this helped him and others in the administration implement the policies and then stay the course. The group was called the President's Economic Policy Advisory Board (PEPAB). It was created in February 1981. As Reagan adviser Martin Anderson, who originally came up with the idea, explained, PEPAB could be "called upon if Reagan's economic program started to veer off the track." Reagan appointed Milton Friedman, Alan Greenspan, Arthur Laffer, William Simon, Thomas Sowell, and other distinguished economists to serve on it. He asked George Shultz to chair it and Martin Anderson to run it. Friedman, Laffer, and Sowell had written widely on the importance of economic freedom and were committed to it. Greenspan, Simon, and Shultz were also committed and had experience as top economic officials in government in the 1970s and had learned important lessons as they saw those principles thwarted. This group met frequently—five times during the first year of the Reagan administration—and helped Reagan resist inevitable pressures to change course.

Another reason why the Reagan administration was

able to implement and adhere to the basic principles was that many of these same people were active in the 1980 presidential campaign. They had worked with Reagan on his economic strategy, so they were ready to go with plans and people as soon as the votes were counted on November 4. Less than two weeks later, on November 16, 1980, many of the economists who had worked together in the campaign wrote an extraordinary memo to Reagan entitled "Economic Strategy for the Reagan Administration." It began with a call for action: "Sharp change in present economic policy is an absolute necessity. The problems . . . an almost endless litany of economic ills, large and small, are severe. But they are not intractable. Having been produced by government policy, they can be redressed by a change in policy."

The memo then outlined a set of reforms for tax policy, regulatory policy, the budget, and monetary policy. There were no temporary tax rebates, short-term public works projects, or other so-called stimulus packages. Rather there were sentences like "The need for a long-term point of view is essential to allow for the time, the coherence and the predictability so necessary for success." You could read George Shultz's quip about economists' lags and politicians' nightmares between the lines.

Importantly, the memo stressed the importance of getting the right people to carry out the policies as much as it stressed implementing the right policies: "able people who served on the [campaign] task forces are available to provide further detail and backup information to you or your designees." Of course, George Shultz and Milton Friedman were two of the authors of that memo.

Monetary Policy Too

One of the most courageous and principled economic officials responsible for restoring the new rules-based, market-oriented, predictable policy was not appointed by Reagan. Paul Volcker took over as chairman of the Federal Reserve Board on August 6, 1979. President Carter's decision to replace the ineffective and weak Fed chairman, G. William Miller, whom Carter had appointed only recently, with Paul Volcker came as a relief to the markets, and to those interested in restoring sound monetary policy. Volcker had the necessary experience as president of the Federal Reserve Bank of New York and as Under Secretary of the Treasury, but more importantly he questioned and publically challenged the view that a higher inflation rate had favorable effects on employment. He was convinced that the opposite was true. He was determined to bring price stability and better economic performance to the Fed.

On September 18, 1979, the Fed approved a ½ percentage point increase in the interest rate it charges banks—the so-called discount rate—in an effort to lower the growth of bank credit and combat inflation. The decision was very close—only 4 votes to 3—which raised doubts about Volcker's leadership and the chance of restoring sound monetary policy. Unfortunately, at first the markets lost confidence in Volcker's ability to lead.

A masterful reversal followed. Soon after the September 18 meeting, Volcker developed a new approach to monetary policy that received the support of every member of the Federal Reserve Board and every Federal Reserve Bank president. It included a full percentage point increase in the discount rate to start fighting inflation; a higher reserve requirement on large banks to restrain lending; and a new operating procedure that emphasized money growth and would allow the interest rate to rise by very large amounts if needed to fight inflation. All these changes were unanimously agreed to and then announced on October 6.

In fact, the interest rate called for by the new operating procedure got extraordinarily high—the peak short-term rate set by the Fed shot up to 19 percent in 1981. Thirty-year fixed mortgage rates rose to 18.5 percent. The economy was hurting and unemployment was rising, an unfortunate but temporary by-product of the new policy. Volcker and his colleagues showed a great degree of fortitude. Mail arriving at the Fed included two-by-fours sent from members of the construction industry furious that homes weren't being built because of the high interest rates. Angry farmers circled the Fed building in Washington. To the builders, the farmers, and many others, the economy was in crisis. Nevertheless, Volcker stayed the course. When asked on *Face the Nation* when he would change from "fighting inflation to fighting unemployment," he answered, "I don't think we can stop fighting inflation. I think we've got to keep our eye on that inflationary ball."

Volcker and his colleagues were resolute, and their efforts paid off. Inflation slowed dramatically, from a peak of 14.6 percent in March 1980, to 8.9 percent in December 1981, and to 3.8 percent by the end of 1982. This reduction in inflation helped set the stage for two decades of steady, strong economic growth. Both knowledge of the economic principles and commitment to the principles were essential. Volcker understood the economic forces that were causing the rising inflation rate through much of the 1970s. But implementing a solution required leadership, including coalition-building. He designed the new procedure to receive wide support at the Fed, and he succeeded. He utilized his technical knowledge of financial markets and banks' reserve requirements. Most importantly, Volcker's plan meant having to stay the course through very difficult times.

What did President Reagan and his economic advisers say about these principles being followed at the Fed? With the 1982 midterm elections looming and unemployment rising, one might have expected them to pressure the Fed to back off those principles and lower interest rates to get the economy moving. But President Reagan was just as resolute as Volcker. He did not pressure Volcker at all. He stuck to the principles and stayed the course despite the political costs. In comparison with the political pressure put on Chairman Martin by the Johnson administration and on Chairman Burns by the Nixon administration, the decision to support Volcker was remarkable.

After reappointing Volcker as Fed chairman in 1983, Reagan named Alan Greenspan to be chairman in 1987. Greenspan would continue the approach started by Volcker, and showed that it was possible to have continued strong growth without inflation. The period of economic stability now known as the Great Moderation was the result.

Parachuting into the Winds

By and large, the winds of economic freedom kept blowing in Washington through the 1980s and continued into the 1990s, but this didn't just happen by itself. I spent another stint at the Council of Economic Advisers during the George H. W. Bush administration, this time as a member. I could see the pressures to move in an interventionist direction after Reagan left town. The most controversial fiscal policy shift, of course, was the compromise by President Bush to increase taxes, after he had campaigned and promised that he would not. But even though this was a big compromise, it was the exception to what otherwise was a continuation of steady-as-you-go policy begun nearly a decade earlier.

To bolster the rules-based approach to monetary and fiscal policy, Bush's Council of Economic Advisers—Michael Boskin, Richard Schmalensee, and me—decided to promote the idea in the *Economic Report of the President*. We wanted to tell people in the new administration and elsewhere about the benefits of rules-based policies without scaring them off. This required explaining that activism had indeed declined in the 1980s and that the economy was better off for it. This was particularly difficult because the economy was drifting into a recession and there were demands both inside and outside the administration to intervene with either monetary or fiscal policy stimulus.

The 1990 *Report* noted that economic performance in recent years had been good because the Fed had "not regressed to an undisciplined, ad hoc approach to policy . . . a purely discretionary approach." Rather it had "attempted to develop a more systematic, longer run approach." Policies should be designed to "work well with a minimum of discretion . . . [T]he alternative to discretionary policies might be called systematic policies . . . Unpredictable changes in economic and financial relationships imply that appropriate policy rules in some circumstances are rather general."

I wrote that section along with the very helpful assistance of Brian Madigan, who was on leave from the Monetary Affairs Division of the Federal Reserve, and others on the staff. The language of Council reports must be vetted throughout the administration and the Fed; so effectively this language, approved by the Fed, represented administration policy. Our work on rules-based policy in that *Report* was featured in the *Wall Street Journal* in an article by David Wessel titled "A Bush Economist Is Urging Hands Off," and they put my picture on the front page to illustrate it.

Toward the end of the Bush presidency, the recession and the nearing election brought calls for more temporary Keynesian stimulus packages, but none were enacted. In 1992, President Bush proposed a very small stimulus—including shifting only $10 billion of government spending from 1993 to 1992, but Congress did not approve it.

The extent to which temporary stimulus measures had fallen into disfavor is evident from President Clinton's first year in office. That year, Clinton proposed a $16 billion stimulus plan. Congress rejected that too and then turned its attention instead to longer-term issues such as reducing the deficit by cutting the growth in spending and raising taxes, and welfare reform, which relinquished some power to the states. Clinton's famous quote that "the era of big government is over" from his 1996 State of the Union address captured well the overall efforts by many in Congress—Newt Gingrich was the Speaker of the House—and the administration to keep the principles of economic freedom alive. So did his less-quoted offer later in the speech when he said, "I will sign immediately" a welfare reform bill that restored incentives to work.

Who Revived Keynesian Activism?

After being largely out of use and out of favor for over two decades, Keynesian activism arose from the dead in the 2000s. It started in the George W. Bush administration and reached unprecedented heights in the Barack Obama administration.

In retrospect, it started with a whimper rather than a bang when a temporary stimulus was added, as part of the Economic Growth and Tax Relief Reconciliation Act of 2001, to the permanent reduction in personal income tax rates that President Bush proposed during the 2000 campaign. These permanent cuts in tax rates were part of an economic plan Bush developed in 1999 as he was deciding to run for president. I was one of the economic advisers to Bush in this campaign and can attest that temporary tax rebates were not part of that plan. In the end, the 2001 act phased in the rate reductions more slowly than the original Bush proposal and added the temporary rebate. In both these respects, the final package tilted in the Keynesian interventionist direction: compared to the original proposal it was more temporary, less permanent.

The tax rebate was up to a maximum of $300 for single filers with no dependents, $500 for single parents, and $600 for married couples. The onetime payments totaled $100 billion, including the $85 billion charged to tax reduction and the $15 billion to spending increases because some of the tax credits were paid in cash if people owed no taxes.

How did this first step in what would turn out to be a revival of Keynesian activism come about? Back-channel efforts by Paul O'Neill, the Secretary of the Treasury, triggered the shift. O'Neill was not involved in the development of the Bush tax cut proposal during the campaign, and he was not enthusiastic about it. He did not like the idea of reducing revenue on a permanent basis, at least not as large a reduction as was proposed. He was concerned that permanent tax cuts would increase the deficit down the road. I know this from conversations with him as the incoming Under Secretary of the Treasury for International Affairs. I told O'Neill that I was in favor of the permanent tax cuts, but my responsibilities were in the international area now. If government spending did not increase as a share of GDP, then the budget could be balanced with the tax cut.

In order to reduce the overall size of the package, and thus its long-term effect on the deficit, O'Neill started talking about reducing the size of the permanent part of the tax cut and increasing the temporary part. This would have the effect of reducing the overall size of the tax cut. Such an idea had some political appeal because the economy went into a recession in March 2001 and created a need for politicians to "do something." But O'Neill could not convince the President or his White House economic advisers, Larry Lindsey and Glenn Hubbard, who also worked on the permanent tax cut proposal in the campaign. Instead, in a meeting with senators in the Dirksen Senate Office Building in March 2001, O'Neill let it be known that "I have about $125 billion of surplus in the Treasury's checking account. Why don't you just use that for an immediate tax rebate?" O'Neill's plan was that by appealing to Keynesian stimulus ideas, he might replace, or at least partly replace, the permanent rate cuts with these temporary rebates.

The White House did not appreciate O'Neill's conversations on Capitol Hill. President Bush had been arguing, correctly in my view, that permanent marginal tax rate cuts would stimulate the economy. President Bush, speaking in Kalamazoo, Michigan, on March 27, made it very clear that "our economy needs more than a pick-me-up, more than a one-time boost."

Nevertheless, in the end, the rebates were passed, along with more permanent tax cuts, and we had a revival of Keynesian countercyclical policy after nearly a quarter century's absence. Once passed and signed, President Bush supported the full package, including the stimulus payments. He even asked O'Neill to get the stimulus checks out rapidly, which he did, driving the Treasury staff to their limits.

O'Neill was asked to resign in December 2002. He was replaced by John Snow, former CEO of CSX. Snow has a Ph.D. in economics from the University of Virginia. He was certainly not a Keynesian activist, and his free-market leanings were more in sync with the principles of economic freedom. Snow was highly effective in selling the second tranche of the more permanent Bush tax cuts—including the cut in the tax rate on capital gains and dividends in 2003.

Who Brought Monetary Activism Back?

The 2001 tax rebate was a departure from steady-as-you-go policy, but the decision by Alan Greenspan to deviate in 2003–2005 from the predictable rules-based policy that worked well in the 1980s and 1990s was much bigger. The deviation was as large as those that occurred in the 1970s. For many years, Volcker and then Alan Greenspan had focused on keeping inflation down and on changing the interest rate in a predictable way, as we explained in the 1990 *Economic Report of the President*.

There is no evidence that Greenspan's decision was a compromise of principle forced by political considerations, as we saw happen in the 1970s. Though my responsibility lay elsewhere, I was close to Alan Greenspan, had lunch with him often, and ran into him at G7 or G20 meetings. I observed no such pressure. And Greenspan did not deviate for any of the reasons he compromised in the case of the 1975 rebate nearly thirty years earlier. Rather it was a clear purposeful decision to deviate from the policy that had served him and the country so well for nearly two decades.

It was his desire to do even better, in my view, which had the unintended consequence of doing worse. It was as Milton Friedman said in his earlier criticism of monetary activism: "The best is often the enemy of the good

. . . The attempt to do more than we can will itself be a disturbance that may increase rather than reduce instability." Greenspan was concerned about the possibility of deflation—a fall in average prices—and possible harmful effects on economic growth as had appeared to happen in Japan in the 1990s. This concern is evident in Federal Open Market Committee (FOMC) meeting transcripts and in the work of the Federal Reserve staff, including that by John Williams, a former Ph.D. student of mine who later would become president of the Federal Reserve Bank of San Francisco. At the January 2002 FOMC meeting, for example, the staff reported that "the economy can become severely destabilized if significant deflation sets in." By deviating from the policy he followed in the 1980s and 1990s, holding interest rates extra low and raising them extra slowly, Greenspan hoped to reduce the risk and increase economic stability.

It was a big departure for Greenspan, and a newly appointed member of the Federal Reserve Board, Ben Bernanke, made a huge difference. Bernanke was known as "helicopter Ben" because he talked about how to stop deflation, or at least how to reduce the risk of deflation, by massive increases in the supply of money. But in a general and more fundamental way, Bernanke was far more of an activist by inclination than Greenspan. For one thing, he came out of the school of economic thought that emphasized interventionist policy à la Samuelson, in contrast to the use of predictable rules à la Friedman.

I observed Bernanke's fondness for activism in a meeting in 1992 in Cambridge, Massachusetts. It was the same year that I presented a paper containing what would come to be called the Taylor rule—a predictable procedure for setting interest rates that has now been used by many central banks. At that Cambridge conference, I was assigned to critique a paper written by Ben Bernanke and Frederic Mishkin, an MIT-trained economist who would join Bernanke on the Federal Reserve Board many years later. Their paper raised doubts about the use of rules for policy instruments; it made the case for a considerable amount of discretion in monetary policymaking. They said that "monetary rules do not allow the monetary authorities to respond to unforeseen circumstances." They were not against the idea of targeting *goals* for monetary policy— such as the inflation rate or the price level. They were criticizing rules for the policy *instruments*—the growth rate of the supply of money or the interest rate. They wanted policymakers to have discretion to do whatever it takes with their instruments of policy to achieve those goals. I dissented strongly from that view in my critique of their paper, probably more strongly than I have ever criticized a paper, referring to all of the research that showed the value of policy rules in which the instruments of policy would adjust in a reasonably predictable way to contingencies.

After Bernanke joined the Federal Reserve Board as a governor, but before he was appointed chairman, he wrote a paper on the Great Moderation, arguing that monetary policy was a significant factor in the improvement in economic stability in the 1980s and 1990s. I showed the Bernanke paper to Milton Friedman, because Milton and I had been arguing for some time about something I had devised called the Taylor curve, which shows that there was a trade-off in which too much price stability would entail a reduction in output stability. Milton was wary of how the Taylor curve might be used by policymakers. He worried that it would encourage fine-tuning, with the central bank departing from basic monetary policy principles. I disagreed, saying that the Taylor curve showed the benefit of rules-based policy because such policy would shift the curve in a more favorable direction. It need not be used to justify activism. Because Bernanke, a current policymaker, used the Taylor curve in the paper, I thought it would give us an indication of how the Taylor curve was being used by policymakers in practice. I was probably not fully objective in assessing Bernanke's paper because I was naturally pleased that he was using my research. But Milton was objective, and his reaction was unequivocal: "John, this is exactly what I mean. In this paper you see a policymaker with an activist bent making use of your curve to justify that activism."

When Bernanke replaced Greenspan in 2006, and especially in the months immediately before, during, and after the financial crisis in 2008, we saw monetary activism as it never had been seen before in the United States. Bernanke used the Fed's resources in a highly discretionary way to bail out the creditors of financial firms. He coordinated with the administration and the Treasury to a degree that made William McChesney Martin look like a piker as he coordinated with the Johnson administration in the late 1960s. Bernanke expanded the Fed's portfolio by unprecedented amounts. He purchased huge amounts of mortgage-backed securities and massive amounts of Treasury securities. He and his compatriots—Henry "Hank" Paulson, the Treasury Secretary, and Timothy Geithner, the president of the Federal Reserve Bank of New York, who succeeded Paulson as Treasury Secretary—did little to articulate a predictable strategy in their bailout policy.

The annual meeting of the world's financial leaders in Jackson Hole, Wyoming, each August illustrates how radically things had changed since Volcker wrestled monetary policy back from the brink in the early 1980s. I attended the first monetary policy symposium in August 1982 and was there for the thirtieth meeting in August

2011. The Tetons were still there, but virtually everything else was different. Volcker attended the meeting in 1982; Bernanke, in 2011.

At the 2011 conference, anticipations ran high that Bernanke would say something in the opening address that would move the markets. Some even attributed stock-market movement in the days before the meeting to rumors that he would hint at new interventions, like a third round of "quantitative easing" or a new "Operation Twist" to lengthen the maturity of the Fed's Treasury portfolio.

The economy was a mess in August 1982, though a different kind of mess than in August 2011. Largely because of those economic woes, a Gallup poll showed an approval rating of only 42 percent for President Ronald Reagan. President Barack Obama's rating in 2011 was even lower, at 38 percent. Interest rates were still very high in 1982: thirty-year fixed-rate mortgages were at 16 percent, compared to 4.2 percent in 2011, and the federal funds rate was over 10 percent. The unemployment rate was 9.8 percent in 1982 and still rising; it would reach a peak of 10.8 percent in November, the trough of that very deep recession.

As I recall the 1982 meeting, it was clear to everyone that Volcker had a policy strategy in place: it was to focus on price stability, despite high and rising unemployment, and thereby get the inflation rate down. This would then restore economic stability and sustainable growth, create jobs, and eventually reduce unemployment. The inflation rate had already been cut in half at the time of the meeting. So unlike Bernanke, Volcker didn't need to use Jackson Hole to announce a new policy intervention. It was clear that he had a strategy.

The 2008 Stimulus Package

Although the 2001 stimulus package had little effect, the Bush administration went back to the Keynesian fiscal policy approach when the economy slowed again in 2007. As a result, Congress passed and President Bush signed into law the stimulus package of 2008. So the winds of economic freedom were really waning now. But why?

Something was different in 2008 compared with the 1980s, when virtually all economists in the Reagan administration as well as Reagan's outside economic advisers shunned short-run stimulus ideas. And something was different from 2001, when Treasury Secretary O'Neill was the only one on the Bush economic team who favored the Keynesian stimulus approach, and therefore had to make an end run around the rest of the team. Instead, in 2007 all of the economic officials in the Bush administration embraced Keynesian ideas. Hank Paulson, the Treasury Secretary who came from Wall Street to replace free-market economist John Snow, was for a stimulus package. So was Edward Lazear, the chairman of the Council of Economic Advisers. By all accounts, so was Ben Bernanke over at the Federal Reserve.

The November 2006 midterm elections, which gave the Democrats control of both the House and the Senate, also created a bully pulpit, or at least a prominent seat at the table, to other people who supported temporary Keynesian packages. Most notable of these was Lawrence Summers, the brilliant and outspoken Keynesian economist, former Treasury Secretary under President Clinton, and former president of Harvard. In a widely covered speech at the Brookings Institution in Washington in December 2007, Summers got out in front of the Bush administration in proposing a new Keynesian stimulus package. He repeated the proposal at a meeting of Congress's Joint Economic Committee, emphasizing what would become the mantra of the revival of Keynesian activism: "A stimulus program should be timely, targeted and temporary." In much the same way that Walter Heller and James Tobin made the case for Keynesian activism in the 1962 *Economic Report of the President*, Keynesian economists advising the Bush administration and Congress were making the case for its revival. The Keynesian approach was now out in the open, not behind closed doors as in 2001, and strongly pushed by the new Democratic Congress and the Republican administration.

The return to activism was not a result of a compromise of principles in order to get something else or to prevent something worse. Rather it was a change in attitude by economic officials and those they advised about the importance of the principles of economic freedom. At the time of the apparent change in attitudes in 2007 and the start of the new interventions, the economy was no worse than it was at the start of the Reagan administration, or for that matter during the slowdowns and recessions during the Great Moderation. The unemployment rate was 4.8 percent in February 2008 when the 2008 stimulus act was passed. It was 7.5 percent in January 1981 when President Reagan entered office.

The Bush economic stimulus did not stave off the downturn or the high unemployment. The panic in the fall of 2008 turned a mild recession into a great recession. The economy actually grew in the second quarter of 2008, but then plummeted by 9.2 percent in the fourth quarter. People naturally blamed President Bush, and through him his fellow Republican and presidential candidate John McCain, for the terrible economic situation. With the economy in such bad shape, Barack Obama easily won the presidency with the promise of making a change.

Doubling Down

But the new administration did not reverse the slide away from economic freedom. It accelerated it. A huge temporary stimulus package was passed in February 2009, which had many of the same features as the 1970s stimulus packages. Many other interventions in fiscal and monetary policy followed. The economists who President Obama brought to Washington were from the same activist schools of thought as those whom they replaced. Christina Romer, with a Ph.D. from MIT, was chosen to chair the Council of Economic Advisers. Larry Summers was chosen to direct the National Economic Council. Ben Bernanke was reappointed to chair the Federal Reserve. And the major Keynesian economists who were cheering from the sidelines—Nobel Prize–winning economists Paul Krugman and Joseph Stiglitz—dared the new Obama appointees to effect even more intervention. Many were students of Paul Samuelson, or students of students of Paul Samuelson, who recruited the economists who first brought Keynesian activism to Washington in the 1960s. Again there was no compromise of principles here that explains the differences from the 1980s; the attitude toward the principles was different from that in the 1980s.

Joining in the cheering and the daring—remarkably echoing the debates of the 1960s—was Paul Samuelson, who said in early 2009 before he passed away, "And today we see how utterly mistaken was the Milton Friedman notion that a market system can regulate itself. We see how silly the Ronald Reagan slogan was that government is the problem, not the solution. This prevailing ideology of the last few decades has now been reversed. Everyone understands now, on the contrary, that there can be no solution without government. The Keynesian idea is once again accepted that fiscal policy and deficit spending has a major role to play in guiding a market economy. I wish Friedman were still alive so he could witness how his extremism led to the defeat of his own ideas."

The Chicago versus Cambridge geographical dichotomy of the 1960s no longer adequately captures the policy differences between the two schools of thought. The Chicago, Harvard, and MIT economics departments evolved in diverse directions, with research differences as large within the departments as between the departments, and with much research taking place at other universities in the United States and other countries. More general geographic terms used to describe the two schools of thought, such as "fresh water" for Chicago and "salt water" for Cambridge, also fail to capture the real policy differences in the Internet age when people can collaborate whether or not they co-locate. The main difference is not where economists studied or where they work, nor even what type of model they use. Rather it is classic "rules versus authorities" dichotomy, or, even broader, the degree of adherence to the principles of economic freedom.

The Obama administration did reach out to other economists. I know that because Christy Romer called me in December 2008 to ask about whether they should enact a temporary stimulus. I advised no, and recommended an alternative plan I had presented the month before to the Senate Budget Committee. I described it as a "permanent, pervasive, and predictable, " policy that would help increase economic growth, rather than yet another "temporary, targeted, and timely" one.

Lessons Learned

I showed in the previous chapter that economic prosperity comes and goes as adherence to the principles of economic freedom comes and goes. In this chapter I told the stories of how people who support and apply the principles of economic freedom come and go over the years. The cast is nonpartisan. The road away from economic freedom in the 1960s and 1970s was taken by Republican and Democratic administrations alike, as was the road back in the 1980s and 1990s, and the reversal in the 2000s.

For citizens interested in restoring prosperity, the lesson is to find and select leaders who, along with their advisers, are most firmly committed to the principles of economic freedom and who know how to implement and maintain them, regardless of political party. In the following chapters I apply the principles to our current predicament and obtain practical solutions ready for these leaders to implement in practice.

3

* * * * *

Defusing the Debt Explosion

Nothing better signifies America's recent failure to follow the principles of economic freedom than the exploding debt of the federal government. I do not exaggerate when I use the word "exploding." Take a look at the line in the debt chart on the next page, developed from Congressional Budget Office (CBO) data. Its soaring upward climb resembles the fireworks on America's Independence Day. But rather than remind us of America's founding, it portends America's ending. I carry a version of the chart in my wallet and show it to my students, and to my children and grandchildren, because it's their future that's on the line. I once published this graph in the *Wall Street Journal*, and people ask me about it more than any other.

The graph shows the total amount of debt owed by the U.S. government to people at home and abroad. When measured in dollars, the debt is so large ($12,500,000,000,000.00 or $12.5 trillion in 2012) that no one can really fathom it, so economists have devised a more meaningful way to look at it. They measure the debt relative to the size of the economy, or, as in this chart, as a percentage of gross domestic product (GDP)— the amount of goods and services the economy produces

From America's Founding to Its Ending?
Federal Debt Relative to the Size of the Economy

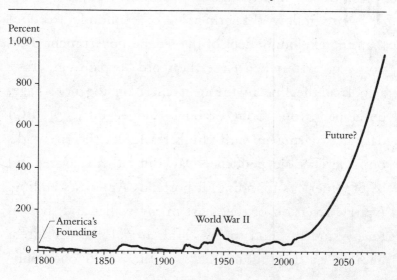

each year and a popular measure of the size of the economy. More production means more income, so GDP also measures the resources American taxpayers have available to service government debt.

The debt percentage offers a gauge of the economy's fiscal health. When the percentage gets too high, problems loom.* There is no hard and fast threshold number that applies in all cases, but historical data show that when a country's debt tops 60 percent of GDP, economic growth declines and the risk of a financial crisis increases. When European countries formed their Economic and Monetary Union (EMU) in 1999, they pledged to keep their debt percentages below 60 percent. The limit was a response to the lessons of history. Unfortunately, many of them, most notably Greece, violated that rule, leading Europe into a major financial crisis.

---

* To understand the debt problem, you don't have to calculate the percentages, like you had to in high school. You just have to use them, like you use a thermometer. A person with a debt of $40,000 and an annual income of $100,000 would have a 40 percent debt ratio. A person with the same debt and an annual income of $40,000 would have a 100 percent debt ratio and would have a tougher time servicing the same-sized debt. The gauge applies to countries as well as people. So when comparing debt over time in America or any other country, measuring the debt as a percentage of the nation's annual production makes sense.

The Shadow of Things That May Be

My debt graph starts at America's founding in the late 1700s and traces the country's fiscal history to the present. But the line in the graph then extends through most of the twenty-first century. The future years represent a projection by the CBO of the debt ratio if America does not put its fiscal house in order. As Scrooge asked in Charles Dickens's classic tale, we must ask ourselves, "Are these the shadows of the things that Will be . . . or are they the shadows of things that May be."

For most of U.S. history, government debt has remained a reasonably healthy percentage of our productive capacity. In years when spending by the federal government rose above tax revenues, it ran a deficit and borrowed money, thereby increasing the debt. In years when government spending fell below revenues, it ran a surplus, and the debt declined as we were paying it off. When the government held spending equal to revenues—balanced the budget—it did not have to borrow and the debt stopped growing. In periods of rapid economic growth, the debt declined relative to the overall size of the economy.

During major wars, the debt rose rapidly simply because defense spending expanded well beyond revenues. In the last two years of World War II, the debt ratio rose to over 100 percent. When the war came to a close, responsible economists warned that the debt must come down. In 1949 at the annual meeting of the American Economic Association, Paul Douglas, the University of Chicago economist who had just been elected U.S. senator from Illinois (after enlisting at age fifty in the Marine Corps and earning two Purple Hearts in the Pacific), gave a speech titled simply "The Federal Budget." He knew the Keynesian stimulus arguments for increased spending and larger deficits, but he was concerned about the large debt: "The problem of balancing the budget and of adopting a sound fiscal policy is not merely economic. It is to an even greater degree a moral issue. We shall need a proper sense of values and a high degree of ethical self-restraint if we are to reach our goal." In part owing to such pleas, but also to strong growth of GDP, the debt percentage came down dramatically. It then fluctuated around 40 percent—equaling 41 percent at the end of the 1980s and 39 percent at the end of the 1990s. Douglas's moral argument resonates today as it appears that the current generation may be passing on a large debt burden to future generations.

Clear and Present Dangers

The World War II debt explosion looks quaint compared with the mountain of debt looming in the future.

Spending has grown to be much larger than revenues in recent years. In 2011 federal spending was $3.6 trillion and revenues were $2.3 trillion. As a result, the deficit—the difference between spending and revenues—was $1.3 trillion, or 9 percent of GDP, about the same percentage as in 2010. The federal government is so deep in the debt hole that it has to borrow more than one-third of what it spends. And it is expected to stay in the hole; the budget will remain in deficit and then the deficit will actually increase in later years if policy is not changed.

At a projected 75 percent in 2012, the debt has already surpassed the worrisome 60 percent of GDP threshold. By the end of this decade it will be passing the 100 percent mark, and if we do not mend our ways, it will grow and grow to over 900 percent! Given these numbers, it was hard to complain credibly when the credit rating firm Standard & Poor's downgraded the U.S. government debt in 2011, even though that firm had lost credibility for poor assessments in the past.

The federal government is clearly not living within its means, and it reflects a failure to apply the principles of economic freedom outlined in chapter 1: to provide a predictable policy framework with rules that prevent politicians from passing legislation to increase spending without building in the means to pay for it, to limit the scope of government, to provide incentives for government officials to spend taxpayers' funds wisely, to rely more on the private sector. And the abandonment of economic discipline is a threat to political freedom as well, for if the fireworks graph is realized, it will be the end of America as we know it. The United States would be an impoverished debtor nation. Interest payments alone, largely to foreign countries, would rise to over 40 percent of GDP, imposing an incredible tax burden on future generations. And we would still be issuing vast sums of debt just to pay that interest.

The growing debt increases the risks of a financial crisis of the kind seen in Europe in 2011 and in many emerging-market countries in the 1990s. It thereby puts us at risk of another deep recession with further unemployment. Adding to the uncertainty, it also risks sustained future inflation, which history shows is caused by too much government borrowing. And it puts firms and consumers at risk of much higher tax rates to generate the revenues to service the debt in the future. Facing such risks, firms hold back on investment and job creation. Our foreign policy also suffers as American financial officials have to beg the Chinese or rich oil-producing countries to buy our debt: creditors have a way of getting you to do things you would not otherwise do.

If we could effectively address the debt problem, the economic benefits would be enormous. We would cre-

ate an environment in which business firms, workers, and
consumers stimulate the economy; higher and more sustainable economic growth would result as we remove the
threats of higher inflation, higher tax rates, higher interest rates, and another major fiscal crisis—all impediments
to private investment and economic growth.

The Elements of a Sound Budget Strategy

Our highest priority should be to end high deficits and
the explosive growth of debt. The good news is that we
can still correct the situation and return to sound fiscal
policy with a balanced budget. But what can concerned
citizens do about it? Americans are looking for the same
commonsense approach to their government's financial
difficulties as they seek from personal financial advisers,
like Suze Orman, Clark Howard, Jane Bryant Quinn, or
even Ben Franklin. The answer is really just as simple:
Get your spending into line with a realistic estimate of
your income. Live within your means. While such down-
home advice sensibly leaves the details up to the family
members, or in the case of the federal government, to the
elected and appointed officials whose job it is to serve the
voters, to achieve action and accountability we must be
more specific. We need to translate these simple, sensible
maxims into a comprehensive government budget strat-

egy. So how do we get from gigantic deficits to a balanced budget?

Let's start with how much the federal government is actually spending now, which is about 24 percent when measured as a ratio to GDP. Next let's consider how much the government was spending before the debt started its explosive climb around 2007. In that year spending was 19½ percent of GDP. A commonsense and quite reasonable budget plan would be to insist simply that federal spending be brought down from 24 percent to 19½ percent of GDP and then held there.

It is important to recognize that a plan such as this, which reduces spending as a percentage of GDP, does not necessarily mean that the number of dollars actually spent by the government declines. In fact, under this plan government spending would increase in tandem with GDP. Government spending would grow from $3.5 trillion in 2011 to $3.9 trillion in 2016 to $4.7 trillion in 2021 under the assumption that GDP grows according to the CBO's forecast.

Some people may want to argue that the percentage should be lower, say, 18 percent of GDP, which was what the government spent in the year 2000. If so, they can think of this proposal as a compromise position. The 19½ percent number does not violate the principles of economic freedom, and as we will see, it brings with it another advantage. In any case the 19½ percent strategy should be doable. It is simply limiting government to the size it was before the financial crisis and the recession. It is not what one would call austerity, a term used to describe drastic and sudden declines in spending that would eliminate most essential functions of government that Americans have been accustomed to for generations.

No Need to Increase Taxes

This plan would not require an increase in tax rates on anyone, whether they are investing, starting a business, expanding an existing one, creating jobs, working, or looking for jobs. Thus it would not risk harming economic growth and thereby increasing unemployment further. Indeed, a plan for which there is no need to increase tax rates will offer a welcome certainty to people making investment decisions, which will in turn spur economic growth and job creation.

Economists estimate that with the tax system we have in place now, federal tax revenues will be around 19½ percent of GDP, on average, in future years. A plan that keeps spending around 19½ percent of GDP will have revenues equal to spending, and the budget will balance.

Room for Revenue-Neutral Tax Reform

A proposal to not increase taxes does not imply that anyone likes the current tax system. It has not been overhauled since the 1986 bipartisan tax reform, and it is in need of another overhaul. An essential characteristic of tax reform—one that applied to the 1986 reform—is that it widens the tax base, through reducing complex loopholes and special tax subsidies, while lowering tax rates, which reduces disincentive barriers that are holding back economic growth and income gains. In addition to reducing the complexity of the tax code, the main purpose of tax reform is to spur sustainable economic growth. Thus, tax reform should be *revenue neutral*. In other words, at any given level of current economic activity, the gain in tax revenue as a result of the wider tax base is offset by a loss in revenue from lower tax rates. If the extra revenues from cutting loopholes were used to increase spending rather than to reduce tax rates, then the pro-growth benefits of tax reform would be reduced.

A variety of tax reform proposals fit these criteria, and the best ones adhere closely to the principles of economic freedom, including predictability, an emphasis on incentives, and a limited role for government. One such proposal, originally put forth by Milton Friedman in *Capitalism and Freedom*, still appears frequently in discussions of tax reform, and has been adopted in other countries but not the United States. It is, as Friedman explained, a "flat-rate tax on income above an exemption, with income defined very broadly and deductions allowed only for strictly defined expenses of earning income." Variations of Friedman's reform proposal include two tax rates, rather than one rate, and more generous deductions. All variations lower tax rates, broaden the base, and limit the tax system to raising revenue, not trying to achieve other ends through subsidies.

By holding spending to 19½ percent of GDP, this plan makes room for such revenue-neutral tax reforms. In addition, by spurring higher economic growth, the tax reform will generate additional tax revenues. Indeed, higher economic growth, not increasing tax rates, is the main route through which tax revenues grow.

Step by Step, Bit by Bit

To fully specify the budget strategy, we now need to lay out the year-by-year spending path from 24 percent of GDP to our target, 19½ percent. The next graph, showing federal spending as a share of GDP, illustrates the plan. Starting on the left, it first shows the recent history of federal spending as a percentage of GDP from the year 2000 to the present. It is the history of a spending binge that took federal outlays from about 18 percent of GDP in 2000 to 19½ percent in 2007 to around 24 percent now.

The top line going forward from the present is the spending plan for the federal government first submitted by President Barack Obama in February 2011. As you can see, that plan left the binge in place, with spending inching back up to 24 percent of GDP in 2021.

The alternative pro-growth plan proposed here is shown in the lower line, which brings spending down, as a share of GDP, to the 2007 level, which is marked by the dashed line drawn at 19½ percent in the graph. As you can see, the pro-growth plan does not bring spend-

Toward a Credible Pro Growth Budget

Federal spending relative to the size of the economy

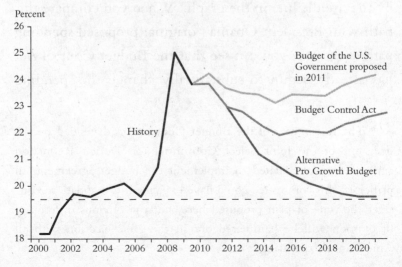

ing down abruptly in one year, or two years, or even five years. Rather it is a very gradual path. It is not a plan to impose austerity. It is simply a plan to undo the recent spending binge in a gradual credible way.

Building on the Budget Control Act of 2011

How can we get started on such a plan? How can it be implemented? Surprisingly there's already a natural starting place: the debt-limit-cum-spending-control agreement reached in the summer of 2011. Signed into law by President Obama on August 2, the Budget Control Act of 2011 has been widely derided as a debacle by both the Left and the Right. Yet it established a base that can be built on. The impact of this plan on spending is illustrated by the middle line in the graph.* When you compare this path with President Obama's original proposed spending path at the top, you can see that the Budget Control Act has already begun to substantially change the spending

---

* The full impact of the Budget Control Act depended on the decisions of the Joint Select Committee on Deficit Reduction appointed and mandated to implement the budget agreement. In principle, this committee could have expanded its mandate to consider the type of plan proposed here, but the obvious differences of opinion will be hammered out in the 2012 election with all Americans participating.

picture. If fully implemented, it would cut federal outlays as a share of GDP to 22 percent in 2021, compared with 24 percent in President Obama's original budget.

The act also, for the first time, limits—or caps—congressional appropriations of spending each year. The legislation states explicitly that appropriations cannot exceed specified dollar amounts each year from 2012 to 2021. If Congress appropriates more than the caps, then automatic reductions take effect in the budget. Excluded from the caps are emergency relief and entitlement spending, yet the caps set a practical legislative precedent that can be adapted to more comprehensive budget plans.

Despite these accomplishments, the 2011 budget agreement does not fully solve the deficit or the debt problem. The plan proposed here finishes the job. As traced in the chart, nothing would change relative to the Budget Control Act until 2014, when spending as a share of GDP starts moving down further, until it reaches the 2007 percentage level in 2019 and thereby allows for fully revenue-neutral pro-growth tax reform.

The gradual nature of the strategy avoids abrupt and unanticipated changes in spending. By bringing spending down gradually as a share of GDP, it does not involve reductions in the number of dollars of federal spending, because GDP is projected by the CBO to grow. The plan only slows overall spending growth. The more credible the strategy is, the greater will be its benefits and the smaller any adjustment costs.

Beyond the Target Path

Legislating a spending path can bring spending growth down, but it does not guarantee it will stay down, as Congress can change the law in the future. We need a longer-term way to restrain special interests. For many years an amendment to the Constitution has seemed like the best answer. Indeed, once the 19½ percent limit is reached, a constitutional amendment linking the growth of spending with the growth of GDP offers the best way forward. Such proposals have been discussed and vetted widely in Congress, and most of the wrinkles have been ironed out. To allow for emergencies, Congress would be able to relax the limit with a greater-than-majority vote of 60 percent of both houses. Automatic reductions in tax revenues during recessions and increases during booms would help stabilize the economy in a predictable way without requiring any temporary changes in legislation.

A truly comprehensive budget strategy will take us toward a more stable and predictable economic policy. It will increase both demand and supply and get the economy growing and creating jobs again. In essence, the strategy starts with a game-changer that excises the spending binge of the past few years before government agencies get used to the new unsustainable spending levels.

What Are the Objections?

People will raise objections to this plan. Some will say we should not take tax increases off the table, and argue for a compromise that includes tax increases and spending reductions. But the reason that the debt is exploding in future years is mainly spending. The often-heard mantra that we have a "spending problem not a revenue problem" is correct. If we raised the tax rate on people in the top tax bracket from 35 to 39.6 percent, as some have suggested, it would increase revenue by less than 1 percent of GDP, and would not change the picture in the fireworks graph in any noticeable way. Underlying that graph is a growth in federal spending that goes to 75 percent of GDP by 2085. About 40 percent of that spending in 2085 is interest payments, but another 35 percent is spending on government programs, compared with 23 percent today. Rapid projected growth in entitlement programs such as Medicare, Medicaid, and Social Security is driving this spending. As we will see, these programs can be reformed to preserve their best features and keep growth below what is projected.

Some critics of this approach say that reducing spending

will decrease economic growth, and among those critics, some argue that we even need another short-term stimulus package to bolster the economy similar to the 2009 effort. The budget consolidation can come later, they say. But as I showed in chapters 1 and 2, these short-term packages have failed. Even their promoters, such as the consulting firm Macroeconomic Advisers run by Laurence Meyer and Moody's Analytics run by Mark Zandi, admit that the effects are temporary and unsustainable. Rather than another Keynesian fiscal stimulus package, we need to transition to a sounder long-term fiscal foundation in a way that promotes growth and creates jobs in the short term but on a sustained basis.

Critics also discount the prospect that a gradual and credible plan to lower spending growth will increase private-sector job creation by reducing the threats of higher taxes, higher interest rates, and a fiscal crisis described earlier in this chapter. In addition, they may not realize that such a plan brings spending down as a share of GDP slowly enough that dollars spent continue to increase from year to year.

Lower government spending as a share of GDP is not associated with higher unemployment. For example, when government purchases of goods and services came down as a share of GDP in the 1990s, unemployment didn't rise. In fact it fell. And the higher level of government purchases as a share of GDP since 2000 has clearly not been associated with lower unemployment. Though correlation does not prove causation, it is hard to see what plausible third factor could reverse this correlation. To the extent that government spending crowds out job-creating private investment, it can actually worsen unemployment. Recent government efforts to stimulate the economy and reduce joblessness by spending more have failed to reduce joblessness.

The stimulating effects of this budget plan would come in part from increased private investment as uncertainty about spending policy and the prospect of higher tax rates is reduced. Higher private investment would lower unemployment. Again, while correlation does not itself prove causation, when private investment is high, unemployment tends to be low. In 2006, investment—business investment plus housing investment—as a share of GDP was high, at 17 percent, and unemployment was low, at 5 percent. By 2010, private investment as a share of GDP was down to 12 percent, and unemployment was up to more than 9 percent. In the year 2000, investment as a share of GDP was 17 percent while unemployment averaged around 4 percent.

Now Is the Time

America needs to get back to living within its means. By doing so, its means will expand dramatically as an economic recovery takes hold and employment and incomes rise. Those of us who are concerned about the recent trends in American economic policy should insist that the candidates we vote for will bring federal spending to what it was as a share of GDP before the crisis and the recession.

This is not austerity. It is reversing the spending binge of the past few years and putting in place reforms that will make government programs work better going forward. To prevent special interests and their lobbyists from eroding these gains after the crisis has passed and growth is again strong, we should limit the scope of government with credible spending growth caps and contingency plans for emergencies.

By design, this plan will not require tax increases. But it does make room for tax reform, which will further the goal of stronger growth. When matched with monetary reform, which I turn to next, it will reduce the risks of financial crises, deflation, and inflation and will put American economic policy back on track.

4

. . . . .

Monetary Rules Work and
Discretion Doesn't

The strong and stable economy of the 1980s and 1990s emerged largely because of a monetary policy that was conducted in a predictable, rule-like manner, with the main goal of reducing inflation and keeping it down. In contrast, monetary policy in the 1970s consisted of a series of unsystematic discretionary increases and decreases in money growth and interest rates that led to high inflation, high unemployment, and low economic growth. In 2003–2005, when the Fed held interest rates too low for too long, it set off excesses in housing and other markets, which brought on the most recent boom and bust. The Fed's continuing departure in recent years from a rules-based monetary policy have increased economic instability and endangered its independence.

The difference in performance between rules and discretion is evident in other countries as well. The European Central Bank held interest rates too low during 2003–2005, and, according to research at the Paris-based Organisation for Economic Co-operation and Development, this decision was a factor in the outsize housing booms in Greece, Ireland, and Spain. These booms in turn sowed the seeds of the busts and the financial crises in these countries, which have created problems for the rest of Europe. As all this was happening in the developed economies of Europe and the United States, emerging-market countries from Brazil to Mexico to Poland were moving away from their chaotic discretionary macro policies of the 1980s and 1990s toward more rule-like policies; the result was improved performance, especially compared with the economies of the United States and Europe.

In the most fundamental sense, the purpose of monetary reform is simple: restore and lock in consistent rule-like policies that work, and avoid discretionary policies that don't. One might hope this goal could be accomplished by appointing central bankers who hold these principles, or maybe hold them more strongly than most people, as Harvard Professor Kenneth Rogoff suggested in a famous academic paper published in 1985. But hard-learned experience suggests that more is needed to prevent monetary policy from veering off track. For this reason, Congress, as part of its responsibility "to coin Money, regulate the Value thereof" under Article I, Section 8, of the Constitution, should take action to permanently prevent the damaging policy swings toward discretion.

More Focus

Basic economic principles and common sense provide our starting point. In any organization, a clear, well-specified goal usually results in a consistent and effective strategy for achieving that goal. Too many goals blur responsibility and accountability, causing decision-makers to choose one goal some times and another goal at other times in an effort to chart a middle course. In the case of monetary policy, multiple goals enable politicians to lean on the central bank to do their bidding and thereby deviate from a sound money strategy.

More than one goal can also cause the Fed to exceed the normal bounds of monetary policy—perhaps veering into fiscal policy or credit allocation policy—as it seeks the additional instruments necessary to achieve multiple goals. There is no justification for an independent agency of government to undertake interventions in these areas. In the spirit of the Constitution, they are best left to

Congress and the President to handle through the regular appropriations process. Central-bank intervention is a poor substitute for sound fiscal policy, and it removes incentives for Congress and the President to do their own jobs well: if the central bank hangs out a "We Do Fiscal Policy" shingle, or is expected to bail out fiscal policy errors, Congress will try to avoid making tough decisions that might harm reelection chances.

Despite these obvious pitfalls, a multiple mandate for the Fed swept in during the great interventionist wave of the 1970s, when Congress passed and President Carter signed into law the Federal Reserve Reform Act of 1977. This new law amended the Federal Reserve Act, which originally created the Federal Reserve in 1913, by explicitly giving the Federal Reserve the goals of promoting both* "maximum employment" and "stable prices." This certainly was the wrong remedy for the inflationary boom-bust economy at the time, and monetary policy worsened for a while.

It was not until Paul Volcker arrived as chairman in August 1979 that things changed. Volcker knew that he had to focus on inflation like a laser beam, despite the dual mandate. Of course, he had to interpret the law in

---

* The act also includes a third mandate, "moderate long-term interest rates," which has received far less attention.

a way consistent with his change in policy. To achieve maximum employment, Volcker would argue, he first had to reduce inflation, even if that increased unemployment in the short run. While that approach eventually served Volcker and the economy well, it also set a precedent that the dual mandate was open to interpretation by the Fed chairman. Alan Greenspan largely continued Volcker's interpretation throughout the 1980s and 1990, but Ben Bernanke and other Fed officials have not.

The first step toward a more consistent policy would be to remove the dual mandate and bring the Fed's focus to a single goal. That goal should be price stability. Monetary policy alone determines the overall price level and thus inflation, the percentage change in the price level, and thus should be responsible for price stability. The ultimate determinant of inflation is the quantity of money in the economy, and Congress has given the Fed the power to control that quantity under Article I, Section 8, of the Constitution. The addition of the dual mandate to the Federal Reserve Act was based on the now-outmoded concept that was popular in the 1970s. Higher inflation, it was thought, would bring about lower unemployment. This notion has since been proved wrong empirically and theoretically.

Single Mandate, Dual Response

To be specific, the section of the Federal Reserve Act pertaining to the Fed's goals (Section 2A) should be repealed and replaced so that the congressional mandate for the Fed is no longer "to promote effectively the goals of maximum employment, stable prices, and moderate long-term interest rates" but rather *to promote effectively long-run price stability within a clear framework of overall economic stability.* The term "long-run" makes it clear that the mandate does not mean that the Fed should overreact to minor ups and downs in inflation in the short run, from month to month or even quarter to quarter. The phrase "within a clear framework of overall economic stability" emphasizes that the single mandate wouldn't stop the Fed from providing liquidity when financial markets freeze up, as they did after the 9/11 terrorist attacks, or serving as lender of last resort to banks during a panic, or reducing the interest rate in a recession.

To better understand what I mean by a "clear framework of overall economic stability," consider a policy rule I proposed in 1992 for the Fed to follow in setting interest rates in order to achieve price stability. Over time the rule has come to be called the Taylor rule—a kind of benchmark for discussing policy. In designing the Taylor rule, I assumed a particular goal for price stability—a target inflation rate of 2 percent per year. But I assumed no long-run employment or GDP goal, in recognition of the fact that the Fed, or any other central bank, does not have the power to affect the level of employment or GDP in the long run, other than through achieving its price stability goal. But under a Taylor rule, the Fed, or any other central bank, is supposed to change its interest rate in response to *both* inflation and GDP. Specifically, the rule says that the Fed should set the interest rate equal to 1½ times the inflation rate, plus ½ times the percentage amount by which the GDP differs from its long-run growth path, plus 1. Thus when inflation rises, the Fed is supposed to raise the interest rate to reduce inflationary pressures and combat the inflation. But, in addition, when there is a recession and GDP declines, the Fed is supposed to cut the interest rate; this helps mitigate the recession and reduce economic instability. In other words, even though there is a single mandate underlying this policy rule, there is a dual response of the interest rate to inflation *and* other variables such as GDP or employment. The dual-response system provides the needed framework of economic stability.

Some Federal Reserve officials worry that a focus on the goal of price stability would lead to more unemployment. But history shows just the opposite. One reason why the Fed kept its interest rate too low for too long in 2003–2005 was the concern that raising the interest rate would risk an increase in unemployment, contrary to the dual mandate. If the single mandate had prevented the Fed from keeping interest rates too low for too long, then it would likely have avoided the boom and bust that played a role in the subsequent financial crisis and led to high unemployment.

But would a single mandate reduce discretion? A quick look at history shows it would. In the years since 2008, the Fed has explicitly cited the dual mandate to justify its unusual interventions, including the bouts of "quantitative easing" from 2009 to 2011, when the Fed purchased massive amounts of mortgage-backed securities and longer-term Treasury securities. During the 1980s and 1990s, Fed officials rarely referred to the dual mandate, even during the period in the early 1980s when unemployment rates were as high as today. When they did so, it was to make the point that achieving price stability was the surest way for monetary policy to keep unemployment down.

Until the recent interventionist period, written policy statements and directives from the Fed never even mentioned the "maximum employment" part of the dual mandate in the Federal Reserve Act. There was not a single reference from 1979, when Paul Volcker took over as Fed chair, until the end of 2008, just as the Fed was about to embark on its first bout of quantitative easing. It increased its references to maximum employment in the fall of 2010 as it embarked on its second bout of quantitative easing.

Still, while a single mandate would have reduced such discretion, it would not have prevented it entirely. Indeed, some, like Greg Mankiw, economics professor at Harvard University, argue that "if the Fed's mandate were different, monetary policy today might well be the same." Thus, despite all of the other advantages of a single mandate, it would be wise to supplement that reform with others.

Writing a Policy Rule into Law

When I proposed a simple policy rule as a guide for monetary policy twenty years ago, I made no suggestion then that the rule should be written into law, or even that it be used to monitor policy, or hold central banks accountable for their actions. The objective was to help central bankers make their interest rate decisions in a more rulelike manner and thereby achieve the goal of price stability within a framework of economic stability. The rule incorporated what we knew at the time from research on the optimal design of monetary rules. In the years since then we have learned much more. We learned that simple rules are robust enough to accommodate widely different views about how monetary policy works. We learned that such rules are frequently used by financial-market analysts looking at monetary policy and by policymakers in their own deliberations. We learned that when policy hews close to such rules, inflation is low, expansions are long, unemployment is low, and recessions are short, shallow, and infrequent; but when policy deviates from such rules, economic performance is poor, with more recessions, higher unemployment, and higher inflation.

This experience has led some monetary scholars and historians—such as the monetary historian Allan Meltzer—to propose that the Federal Reserve be instructed to follow such a rule. A legislated rule could reverse the short-term focus of policy and restore credibility in sound monetary principles.

To see how we might legislate monetary rules, it is useful to look back to the history of legislation relating to the growth in the supply of money, or as different measures of the money supply are sometimes called, "the monetary aggregates." Until the year 2000 the Federal Reserve Act had a specific reporting requirement about the growth of the monetary aggregates. It called for the Fed to submit a report to Congress and then testify in February and July of each year, laying out its plans for money growth for the current and next calendar years.

The legislation required only that the Federal Reserve report its plans for money growth, not that the Fed set the plans in any particular way. The Fed had discretion to choose the growth rates of the aggregates. But if the Fed deviated from the plans, it had to explain why. If Federal Reserve policymakers determined that their reported objectives or plans, according to the words of the act, "cannot or should not be achieved because of changing conditions," they "shall include an explanation of the reasons for any revisions to or deviations from such objectives and plans."

The reporting requirement was fully repealed in 2000 because over time the data on money growth had become less reliable as people found alternatives to money—such as credit cards or money-market mutual funds—for making payments. The Fed subsequently started focusing more on the interest rate rather than money growth when it made its policy decisions. In itself, therefore, it was perfectly reasonable to remove the reporting requirement for money growth in 2000, but the problem was that nothing comparable about interest rate reporting was put in its place. A legislative void concerning reporting requirements, and therefore accountability, opened up. We could say that the reporting-accountability baby was thrown out with the monetary aggregate bathwater.

Political Control without
Day-to-Day Interference

The most straightforward way to legislate a rule for monetary policy would be to fill this void by reinstating the reporting and accountability requirements that were removed in 2000. But rather than focus only on money growth, they could focus directly on the rule-like response of the interest rate.

This proposal would limit the Fed's discretion by requiring that it establish and report on a policy rule for the interest rate. The proposal does not require that the Fed choose any particular rule for the interest rate, only that it establish some rule and report what the rule is.

But if the Federal Reserve deviates from its chosen strategy, the chairman of the Fed must provide a written explanation and answer questions at a public congressional hearing. So while the proposal limits discretion, it does not eliminate discretion. It provides a degree of control by the political authorities without interfering in the day-to-day operations of monetary policy.

What Would Have Happened?

How might have policy differed if Congress had not simply repealed the reporting requirements in 2000 but also replaced them as described here? Considerable empirical work now supports the view that interest rates were too low for too long in 2003–2005 and were a major factor in the housing boom and bust that resulted. I first presented the evidence in the summer of 2007. Many Fed officials—including Ben Bernanke, who was there—were not pleased to hear my findings. That fall, Frank Smets, who directs research at the European Central Bank, presented a paper (which he wrote with his colleague Marek Jarocinski) at a Federal Reserve Bank of St. Louis conference that confirmed my finding with further evidence, concluding that "easy monetary policy designed to stave off perceived risks of deflation in 2002–04 has contributed to the boom in the housing market in 2004 and 2005." In 2010, Rüdiger Ahrend of the Organisation for Economic Co-operation and Development reviewed similar findings in Europe, showing that " 'below Taylor' [meaning interest rates were too low compared to those recommended by the Taylor rule] episodes have generally been associated with the build-up of financial imbalances in housing markets."

But there are different views. Chairman Bernanke, in a speech before the American Economic Association in January 2010, took on my 2007 analysis and argued that if you use a different analysis, the interest rate did not appear to be too low. Bernanke found that when he substituted the Fed's *forecasts of inflation* in a Taylor rule in place of *actual inflation*, the interest rate was not too low in 2003–2005. I replied to his critique in the *Wall Street Journal*, arguing that there are problems with using forecasts, including that they are neither objective nor accurate. Indeed, in the episode in question, the Fed's inflation forecasts were too low compared to what the actual rate was, and even lower than what the private sector was forecasting.

Differences of opinion are not unusual in economics, and it is good to air them in public. But Ben Bernanke gave his explanation years after the decisions were made and long after any debate could have had an impact on them. Were these legislative reporting requirements in place during 2003–2005, the Fed would have had to announce its strategy well in advance, and then if it deviated from the strategy, it would have had to explain why. In my view, such open discussion at the Fed and in Congress would have greatly reduced the extent of policy deviation in the run-up to the crisis.

The same holds true for the period of the crisis when there was little public discussion of the rationale for the interventions undertaken. Had the reporting requirements been in place, we would have had some discussion and debate. That debate would have led to fewer interventions, and any interventions that did manage to get through would have been less extreme and disruptive.

To assess the validity of such a counterfactual hypothesis, we can divide the financial crisis into three periods. The first period runs from August 2007, when the interest rates banks charge each other in the money market started to rise, until late September 2008, when panic set in. The second period is the panic itself. Based on the fall in equity prices and rise in interbank interest rates, the panic period was concentrated in late September through October 2008 and spread rapidly around the world, turning the recession into a great recession. The third period occurs after the panic. Thus the financial crisis and the Fed's actions fall naturally into three periods: pre-panic, panic, and post-panic.

In the first period, the extraordinary measures taken in the lead-up to the panic did not work and some were harmful. John Williams, now president of the Federal Reserve Bank of San Francisco, and I examined, in early 2008, a new intervention designed to get banks to borrow more from the Fed by having them bid anonymously for loans in an auction rather than going to the Fed directly, which might signal they had problems. The objective was to lower the interest rate that banks were charging each other and thus ameliorate the crisis.

Williams and I showed that during this period the facility had little or no effect on interest rates. Worse, in my view, it drew attention away from the serious problem that many U.S. financial institutions held loans and securities that were in a risky and precarious position. Providing loans to banks in this way does nothing to reduce those risks and thus did little to reduce the interest rate they charge each other. The Fed had misdiagnosed the problem, thinking that the banks simply needed loans to tide them over, when in fact they had deeper problems. I think that an open and transparent discussion of the purposes of this program, as would have been required under a good reporting law, would have uncovered these problems.

The extraordinary bailout measures that began with Bear Stearns before the panic were the most harmful interventions. In this case the Fed presented little or no overarching strategy, as some outside commentators had recommended, and its actions quickly became ad hoc and erratic. The Fed's broad justification for the bailout in the case of Bear Stearns led many to believe that the Fed would do the same thing with any similar institution. But when the Fed was unsuccessful in getting private firms to help rescue Lehman Brothers over the weekend of September 13–14, 2008, it surprised everyone and cut off access to its funds, refusing to bail out Lehman's creditors. The next day, it reversed course, reopening its access to rescue the creditors of AIG. Then it turned off access, and a new legislative program, the Troubled Asset Relief Program (TARP), was proposed to Congress and rolled out by Chairman Bernanke and Treasury Secretary Paulson in a confusing way, one that few could understand. The chaotic rollout of the TARP coincided with the severe panic, which lasted several weeks. The Fed's on-again/off-again bailout measures were thus an integral part of a generally unpredictable and confusing government response to the crisis, which, in my view, led to panic.

With reporting requirements in place, the Fed would have had to outline its reason for deviating from normal lender-of-last-resort practice with the program Williams and I investigated, and it would have had to confront alternative views from the outset. When the plan failed, it would have had to explain why. Similarly, with reporting requirements, the Fed would have had to explain the strategy underlying the bailout of Bear Stearns creditors. This in turn would have given the markets and investors a better assessment of what would happen if Lehman were in trouble, thereby reducing the surprise factor when the Fed pulled back.

The panic is the most complex period to analyze because the Fed's main measures during this period—support for money-market mutual funds and the commercial-paper market—were intertwined with bank debt guarantees by the Federal Deposit Insurance Corporation. In addition, on October 13, after three weeks of uncertainty about how the TARP would work, Treasury Secretary Paulson changed the plan and explained that the funds would simply be used to purchase preferred equity shares from the banks, instead of trying to buy bad loans, and thereby provide the banks with more capital. This clarification of how the TARP would work was a major reason for the halt in the collapse of the stock market and the end of the financial panic. In addition, the Fed explained its actions and their purposes during the panic better than it did before the panic, and this helped rebuild confidence, stopping the runs out of money-market mutual funds and stabilizing the commercial-paper market. The Fed should also be given credit for working closely during the panic with central banks abroad, in lending channels and explaining their purpose clearly.

In the post-panic period the Fed unfortunately continued its interventions, including the purchases of more than $2 trillion in mortgage-backed securities and long-term Treasuries. These programs were justified with frequent references to the Fed's dual mandate and to unpublished estimates of the likely size of the impacts. My assessment, based on research with Stanford student Johannes Stroebel, is that the purchase of mortgage-backed securities had at best a small effect on mortgage rates. I think it would have been very difficult to justify these deviations without the dual mandate or with the scrutiny of formal reporting requirements.

Removing the Monetary Overhang

In order to pay for the mortgages and other securities it purchased from banks during and after the financial crisis, the Fed had to create money. But instead of literally printing dollar bills and giving them to the banks in exchange for the mortgages, which would be a logistical nightmare when you are talking about trillions of dollars, the Fed simply credited the banks with electronic deposits—or bank money. That way the Fed would take in, for example, a billion dollars' worth of mortgages from Bank of America, and Bank of America would get a billion dollars of bank money.

The result of the trillions of dollars poured into these purchases has been an enormous and completely unprecedented explosion in the amount of bank money, as shown in the chart on the next page. To provide some perspective, the chart starts in the year 2000. The balance of funds the banks hold at the Fed—this is the so-called bank money—is shown on the vertical axis in billions of dollars. A tiny blip appears on the chart around September 11, 2001, the day of the terrorist attacks. The Fed had to increase the amount of bank money at that time because the attacks on the World Trade Center damaged the payments system and banks needed money to make payments. The Fed wisely and appropriately provided the money. But that amount is completely dwarfed by the recent explosion.

The large recent increase started in the fall of 2008 during the panic. Before the panic the amount was about $10 billion. By the end of 2008 it was $800 billion. By the end of 2011 it was $1,700 billion. In the fall of 2008 the money was used mainly for making loans to U.S. banks, securities firms, and foreign central banks. As the panic subsided, the demand for those loans diminished and the

Bank Money Created by the Fed

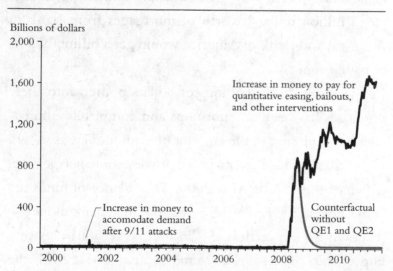

bank money would have retreated back to where it was before the crisis. But instead the Fed started the large-scale purchases of mortgages and Treasury bonds, first under QE1 and then under QE2, which expanded the balances by much more.

This large monetary overhang creates risks to the financial system and the economy. If it is not reduced, then the bank money will eventually pour out into the economy and cause a rise in inflation. But if it is reduced too quickly, the banks may find it hard to adjust and the economy would take a hit. In order to unwind the programs in the current situation, the Fed must sell its mortgages, but no one knows for sure how much mortgage interest rates will rise as the mortgages are sold. Uncertainty also abounds about why banks are holding so much bank money. If the current level is the amount banks desire to hold, then reducing the level could cause a further reduction in bank lending.

For these reasons, as part of its overall monetary strategy, the Fed needs to develop a gradual and credible plan to reduce this overhang. Had it not undertaken QE1 or QE2, it would already have removed the overhang—as shown by the "counterfactual" line in the chart—and there would be considerably less uncertainty about monetary policy down the road.

First Principles

The Road Ahead for the Fed

Many citizens are understandably critical of the Fed's recent interventions, whether bailing out certain financial institutions and not others, reallocating credit from one sector to another, or simply undertaking so many apparently ineffective and confused actions. They are also concerned that the interventions have caused, and are still causing, uncertainty about inflation, deflation, or the future independence of the Federal Reserve. This very uncertainty may be holding back investment and hiring.

The way out of this predicament is not to "end the Fed," as some have urged, but rather to reform the Fed. As we have seen, under such reforms, the Fed should focus on long-run price stability within a clear framework of economic stability. It should also report its strategy and be accountable for deviations from that strategy. To the extent that the deviations entail loans and actions that impact particular firms or markets, they should be subject to audit.

More specifically, the Fed should publish and follow a monetary rule as its means to achieving long-run price stability. Such a rule should include, among other things, a description of interest rate responses to economic developments. It should address how the Fed will achieve those responses through money growth. Within the context of crisis conditions, the Fed should have the discretion to deviate from its stated strategy. However, it should have to promptly report to Congress and to the public the reasons for the deviation. Implementing such a reform will allow Congress to exercise appropriate political control without micromanaging the Fed.

5

Ending Crony Capitalism as We Know It

Keynes: Even you must admit that the lesson we've learned is that more oversight's needed or else we'll get burned.

Hayek: Oversight? The government's long been in bed with those Wall Street execs and the firms that they've led.*

ost Americans are disgusted by the slew of government bailouts in 2008 and 2009. They argue, quite sensibly, that those who created the problems that led to the financial crisis should pay a penalty rather than be bailed out by taxpayers. The very idea that Wall Street benefited as Main Street suffered raises doubts about the American economic system, and adds to people's concerns about the future of the economy. It just doesn't seem fair

---

* From the hip-hop video "The Fight of the Century," by John Papola and Russ Roberts.

that large financial firms and their creditors were bailed out when small businesses were left to fail and families were forced from their homes in foreclosure.

These sentiments have led to calls for legislation that would give the federal government more power and more scope to regulate the economy, not only the banks and the financial markets at the center of the crisis, but other firms and industries as well. In the past few years, politicians have responded to that clamoring and at times even stirred it up. They have enacted new regulations that increase the discretionary power of government in the financial industry through the Wall Street Reform and Consumer Protection Act of 2010, commonly called the Dodd-Frank bill after its sponsors, former senator Christopher Dodd and Representative Barney Frank. The urge for the government to re-regulate and intervene extended well beyond the financial services industry. Building on a long-existing desire in some quarters for national health care, President Obama and the Congress moved major legislation affecting the health care industry, called the Patient Protection and Affordable Care Act of 2010. Other sectors of the economy experienced new interventions by government decree rather than new legislation, such as those by the Environmental Protection Agency (EPA) in the area of carbon emission. This new activism creates increased uncertainty for any firm potentially affected, and raises costs of doing business that may have blunted the economic recovery.

Both the principles of economic freedom and the empirical evidence of what actually has gone wrong in the economy suggest quite clearly that the government did not need more power or more discretion to regulate more markets or more firms in the wake of the crisis. It already had plenty of power before then. Indeed, it was this very power and discretion that led inexorably to the favoritism, to the bending of rules, to the reckless risk-taking, and, yes, to the bailouts. Government bureaucrats chose which existing regulations to enforce and which ones to bend, and they decided who was bailed out and who wasn't. They even went beyond the stated aims of recent interventionist legislation by using funds designated to rescue financial firms to bail out unrelated industries, including automobile companies. This is textbook crony capitalism: the power of government and the rule of men—rather than the power of the market and the rule of law—to decide who will benefit and who will not.

Economists have identified a specific version of crony capitalism that they call regulatory capture: the tendency for regulated firms and their government regulators to develop mutually beneficial relationships that harm the economy, public safety, and people's lives more generally. The benefits to the regulated firms may include lax supervision, protection from competition, or government bailouts. The benefits to the regulators may be lucrative post-government employment, political contributions, or favors to family and friends, which may be implicit or explicit. Of course, the problem of regulatory capture goes beyond heavily regulated industries. For example, many firms have asked for waivers from the new health care legislation, and government officials have the power to decide which ones are granted the waiver. Crony capitalism can exist in any industry in which government policy has a large role, which is the vast and growing majority of industries today.

Regulatory capture and more general crony capitalism caused financial regulatory policy to deviate from rules-based principles and thereby helped cause the crisis. Unfortunately the financial regulations passed in 2010 do little to curb the excesses, and they have not ended the bailout mentality that could push America once again into crisis. Unfortunately the newly passed health care regulations raise costs and contribute to an atmosphere of unpredictability that has slowed down the economic recovery. Fortunately there's a way out, and it's the same way for financial services, health care services, and the whole economy.

Government Regulation of Financial Markets

A remarkably large number of federal and state government agencies, with complex overlapping jurisdictions, regulate the financial sector in the United States. Commercial banks are regulated by the Federal Reserve, the Office of the Comptroller of the Currency, and the Federal Deposit Insurance Corporation (FDIC), as well as by state regulatory agencies. Securities firms are regulated by the Securities and Exchange Commission (SEC). Insurance companies are regulated at the state level. The government-sponsored enterprises that invest in and guarantee mortgages, Fannie Mae and Freddie Mac, are regulated by the Federal Housing Finance Agency (FHFA), which combined the previous Office of Federal Housing Enterprise Oversight (OFHEO) with the Federal Housing Finance Board. The Dodd-Frank bill expanded the Federal Reserve's responsibility beyond bank-holding companies to include all systemically important financial institutions, though the term "systemically important" was never defined.

Global financial firms are also regulated by government agencies in other countries. Supranational groups also provide some international coordination. The Financial Stability Board, for instance, has already designated twenty-nine banking firms (Bank of America, Bank of

New York Mellon, Citigroup, Goldman Sachs, JPMorgan Chase, Morgan Stanley, State Street, Wells Fargo, Barclays, HSBC, Lloyds Banking Group, Royal Bank of Scotland, Credit Suisse, UBS, BNP Paribas, Banque Populaire, Group Credit Agricole, Societe Generale, Santander, Dexia, Nordia, Mitsubishi, Mizuho, Sumitomo Mitsui, Bank of China, UniCredit, Commerzbank, Deutsche Bank, ING) as systemically important.

Excessive Risk-Taking

While the financial industry has long had plenty of eyeballs focused on it, the financial crisis and panic of 2008 revealed serious deficiencies in this regulatory and supervisory process. There is little disagreement that the rules and regulations in place in the years leading up to the crisis were not adequately enforced by the regulators and supervisors in a number of important cases. The most documented cases are Fannie Mae and Freddie Mac. These two giant, private, government-sponsored enterprises support the U.S. housing market by buying mortgages and packaging them into marketable securities, which they then guarantee and sell to investors or add to their own portfolios. Both organizations have been regulated by government agencies with the purpose of preventing them from taking excessive risks. However, by any reasonable measure, both agencies undertook excessive risk starting in the late 1990s when they guaranteed home mortgages that had a high probability of default.

Both the government regulators and the firms they failed to regulate properly share a significant blame for the financial crisis and the global recession. But so do others in government. In both the Clinton and George W. Bush administrations, the Department of Housing and Urban Development (HUD) required Fannie Mae to direct 50 percent of its financing to households that had incomes below the median income for their city or region. This required encouraging some people to take on such loans even though their ability to pay them back was questionable. Thus this policy accentuated the housing boom that led to the financial bust. Obviously the regulators failed in their most fundamental responsibility, and the result was catastrophic.

But Fannie Mae and Freddie Mae were not the only regulated financial institutions that took on excessive risk. Large financial firms from Citigroup to AIG to Bank of America to Bear Stearns to Lehman Brothers—all regulated by government agencies with the stated purpose to prevent excessive risk—were heavily invested in risky securities based on questionable home mortgages or other debt. The wider bank and insurance regulatory system apparently failed as well.

The Capture and the Smoking Guns

What role did regulatory capture have in causing this failure? In the case of Fannie Mae, the evidence of cozy connections with the government is substantial. In their book *Reckless Endangerment, New York Times* reporter Gretchen Morgenson and her colleague Joshua Rosner show that government officials took actions that benefited well-connected individuals, and that these individuals in turn helped the government officials. This mutual-support system thwarted good economic policies and encouraged reckless ones. It thereby helped bring on the crisis, sending the economy into recession.

The government supported Fannie Mae in the form of implicit guarantees, favorable regulatory treatment, and protection from competition. These benefits enabled Fannie to rake in excess profits—$2 billion in excess according to the Congressional Budget Office (CBO). Fannie's executives, such as Jim Johnson, CEO from 1991 to 1998, used the excess profits to support government officials in a variety of ways and had plenty left over for large bonuses, according to the investigative reporting in *Reckless Endangerment*. They got jobs for friends and relatives of elected officials, including Barney Frank. They set up partnership offices around the country that provided more jobs for favored individuals. They financed publications where writers would argue that Fannie's role in promoting homeownership justified federal support and that Fannie was not a serious risk to taxpayers. They persuaded executive-branch officials to ask their staffs to rewrite reports critical of Fannie. They arranged for "sweetheart" loans from Countrywide, the mortgage firm led by Angelo Mozilo, to politicians with power to affect Fannie, such as Senator Chris Dodd. Countrywide partnered with Fannie in originating many of the loans that Fannie packaged (26 percent in 2004).

Some government officials resisted Fannie's lobbying efforts. CBO Director June O'Neill refused to stop the release of a study by CBO staffer Marvin Phaup showing that federal support increased Fannie's profits by $2 billion. O'Neill reported that Fannie executives "Frank Raines and Bob Zoellick came and met with me and the people from CBO. All of us had the same feeling—that we were being visited by the Mafia." Treasury Secretary John Snow proposed the creation of a new more independent regulator in September 2003, but he was unsuccessful in persuading Congress to go along.

Morgenson and Rosner also report on a cozy connection between the Federal Reserve Bank of New York and the Wall Street financial community, focusing on Timothy Geithner (who became president of the New York Fed in 2003) and top Wall Street bankers such as Sanford

"Sandy" Weill, head of Citigroup. At the time, Citigroup was increasing the size of its off-balance sheet and looked overly risky while the New York Fed, for reasons that are still not fully explained, did not stop it, despite having the power to do so. It's very hard to imagine such extreme risk-taking at heavily regulated banks without at least the implicit support of regulators.

Wrong Diagnosis, Wrong Treatment

The Dodd-Frank Wall Street Reform and Consumer Protection Act of 2010 was enacted to prevent another financial crisis, but it misdiagnosed the crisis and enacted the wrong remedies. People are now waking up to the fact that the bill does not do what its supporters claimed. The sheer complexity of the 2,319-page Dodd-Frank bill certainly increases risks to the economy, but when we sift through the many sections and subsections, we find much more than complexity to worry about. Instead of preventing future financial crises, it makes them more likely. And in the meantime it impedes economic growth. Critics on both the left and the right have attacked Dodd-Frank: "The Failure of Financial Reform, Itemized," from John Talbott of the *Huffington Post*; "Phony Financial Reform" from Thomas Donlan of *Barron's*. Congressman Paul Ryan, writing in the *Wall Street Journal*, argued that the bill created a "permanent Wall Street bailout authority." Simon Johnson, former chief economist at the International Monetary Fund, argues that it is an "illusion to think that this solves the problems posed by the impending collapse of one or more global megabanks," and that any Treasury Secretary would circumvent the act and simply bail out the creditors of large financial firms as they did in 2008.

While political factors—special-interest lobbying, social-activist pressures, covering up of past mistakes—were probably behind much of the bill's architecture, economic analysis reveals that it also was based on a misdiagnosis of the financial crisis. As a result, the bill is riddled with deviations from sensible policy. The biggest factor contributing to the misdiagnosis is the presumption that the government did not have enough power to avoid the crisis. It most certainly did. The Federal Reserve had the power to avoid the monetary excesses that accelerated the housing boom and thereby led to defaults, foreclosures, and toxic assets. The New York Fed had the power to stop the questionable lending and trading decisions of Citigroup and others. With hundreds of regulators on the premises of such large banks, it also should have had the information to do so. The SEC could have insisted on reasonable liquidity rules to prevent investment banks from relying so much on short-term funds to finance long-term investments. And the Treasury, in concert with the Fed, had the power to intervene with troubled financial firms.

In fact, during the crisis, Federal Reserve and Treasury power became highly discretionary. They chose to bail out some creditors and not others, to take over some businesses and not others, to let some firms go through bankruptcy and not others. These on-again/off-again policies directly contributed to the financial panic in the fall of 2008.

Instead of trying to implement existing government regulations more effectively and thereby help prevent future crises, the Dodd–Frank bill vastly increases the power of government in ways that are unrelated to the recent crisis and may even encourage future ones. The bill creates a new resolution or "orderly liquidation" authority, in which the FDIC can intervene between any complex financial institution and its creditors in any way it wants to. Effectively, the bill institutionalizes the bailout process by giving the government more discretionary power to intervene. Because the FDIC does not have experience taking over such large complex financial institutions, the government in a state of panic would likely bail them out again. The problem of "too big to fail" remains, and any existing cozy relationship between certain large financial institutions and the government will likely continue. The proposed liquidation process increases the incentive for creditors and other counterparties to run whenever there is a rumor that a government official is thinking about intervening. Who is going to be helped? Who is going to be hurt? It is up to government officials to decide, not the rule of law.

Another false remedy is the new Bureau of Consumer Financial Protection housed at, and financed by, the Fed; the new Bureau will write rules for every type of financial service, most of which have no conceivable connection with the crisis, such as payday loans.

The bill does reduce the power of the Fed to intervene to bail out the creditors of a single financial institution, as the Fed did in the case of Bear Stearns and AIG, but it authorizes such bailouts for creditors of "any participant in any program or facility with broad-based eligibility." In our interconnected financial system, this is hardly a constraint. The bill also gives complete discretion to the Fed and the Treasury to determine "the policies and procedures governing emergency lending."

A new regulation for any firm that used financial instruments to reduce the risks of interest rate or exchange rate volatility offers another example of how off the mark Dodd-Frank ended up. The bill gives the Commodity Futures Trading Commission (CFTC) authority to place margin requirements on such firms even though they had nothing to do with the crisis; their customers and employees will be penalized by the increased costs. And while the bill correctly merges the Office of Thrift Supervision into the Office of the Comptroller of the Currency, it creates more regulatory ambiguity by assigning both the SEC and the CFTC the new job of regulating over-the-counter derivatives with imprecise guidance of who does what.

By far the most significant omission in the bill is its failure to address and reform Fannie Mae and Freddie Mac. Some excuse this omission by saying that it can be handled later, but the purpose of comprehensive reform is to balance out political interests and reach compromise. That compromise will be much harder to reach now that the Dodd-Frank bill is law.

Dodd-Frank also omits a needed reform of the bankruptcy code that would allow large, complex financial firms to go through a predictable rules-based Chapter 11 process without financial disruption and without bailouts. Without this orderly bankruptcy alternative, the "too big to fail" dilemma will not go away. At least the Dodd-Frank bill called for a study of the matter, which may eventually provide an opening for real reform. The good news for those who value economic freedom is that major parts of this "bailout bill" can be repealed and replaced.

Real Financial Reform through Economic Freedom

The extra power given to the federal government through bypassing proven bankruptcy rules looms as the biggest challenge to meaningful reform. Experience shows that such power increases, not decreases, the likelihood of another crisis. You do not prevent bailouts by giving the government more power to intervene in a discretionary manner. You prevent bailouts by requiring adequate capital based on simple, enforceable rules and by making it possible for failing firms to go through bankruptcy without causing disruption to the financial system and the economy.

Fortunately, it is not necessary to provide this additional discretionary authority. Economists and lawyers working with bankruptcy experts, including Thomas Jackson of the University of Rochester, have developed a reform to the bankruptcy law designed especially for large financial institutions. Called "Chapter 14" because there is no such numbered chapter in the current bankruptcy code, its goal is to let a failing financial firm go into bankruptcy in a predictable way without causing spillovers to the economy, and permitting, if possible, people to continue to use its financial services—just as people flew on United Airlines planes, bought Kmart sundries, and tried on Hartmarx suits when those firms were in bankruptcy.

Chapter 14 would differ from the well-known Chapter 7 and Chapter 11 of the current bankruptcy law. It would create a group of "special masters" who are knowledgeable about financial markets and institutions and who would advise and work with the judges; a common perception is that bankruptcy is too slow to deal with the systemic-risk situations in large, complex institutions, but under this proposal there would be capacity to proceed immediately. In addition to the typical bankruptcy commencement by creditors, a government agency could initiate an involuntary proceeding and propose a reorganization plan—not simply liquidation. Debtors and creditors would negotiate, with clear rules and with judicial review throughout the process. In contrast, the orderly liquidation authority of Dodd-Frank offers less transparency, opens the door to capricious discretion by government officials, and provides few opportunities for review in a timely manner. Instead of a government official declaring, "We will wipe out the shareholders" or "It's unfair for us to claw back so much from creditors," under Chapter 14 the rule of law applies. Chapter 14 could also handle the complexities of modern finance—so-called repurchase agreements and derivatives—simply by applying the rules of contracts and procedures already in traditional bankruptcy law with only a few modifications. As George Shultz puts it in the book *Ending Government Bailouts as We Know Them*, "Let's write Chapter 14 into the law so that we have a credible alternative to bailouts in practice."

What are the obstacles to following this sensible advice? One hurdle is that the congressional judiciary committees, rather than the banking committees (which worked on Dodd-Frank), have jurisdiction over bankruptcy law, and it is too hard to coordinate between the two committees. But bureaucratic silos should not get in the way when the stakes are so high.

In the interest of compromise, it would be possible to add a Chapter 14 provision to the Dodd-Frank bill and not repeal its new orderly liquidation authority. The problems with the orderly liquidation authority, at least in the absence of a new bankruptcy process, is that it increases uncertainty, raises constitutional due-process issues, increases the probability of bailouts, and creates moral hazard. If it were on the books, Chapter 14 would give government officials a viable alternative to the current law; they would likely find Chapter 14 more attractive than liquidation or a more direct bailout.

The 2010 Health Care Legislation

While the Dodd-Frank bill neglects many of the principles of economic freedom, the 2010 health care law recklessly ignores and violates them all. At the heart of the new health care law is a mandate that requires Americans to buy health insurance or pay a fine. Several state attorneys general have argued that the Commerce Clause of the Constitution prevents Congress from requiring individuals to purchase particular things. Whether or not they win their argument in the Supreme Court, the mandate obviously runs counter to the basic principles of economic freedom.

The new health care law also creates an Independent Payment Advisory Board of fifteen political appointees who have broad, largely unaccountable powers to control health care markets and health care. The panel's decisions about Medicare become law unless a supermajority of Congress votes to reject its decision. This insulation from meaningful debate makes spending less accountable to the voters, gives more discretion to unelected experts, and abandons the usual checks and balances that make democratic government work. It leaves government officials and well-connected crony capitalists to make decisions for the rest of us, a state of affairs far removed from the principles of economic freedom.

In addition, the 2010 health care law requires that large firms provide health insurance of a particular government-mandated type to their employees or else pay a penalty. As a measure of the cost burdens of this provision, over 1,400 firms have already been granted waivers from its mandates. But these waivers are only temporary, and firms that have the right connections or the funds to lobby government officials may be more likely to get them. This is crony capitalism in the making.

Real Health Care Reform through Economic Freedom

There is a much better way to proceed in reforming health care if we pay attention to rather than ignore the principles of economic freedom. First, let's document with facts what is good about American health care and what needs to be improved.

By many empirical measures the American health care system is excellent, the best in the world in a variety of areas. Scott Atlas, a medical doctor at Stanford University, has shown that "treatment outcomes from the most serious diseases including cancer, cardiovascular disease, stroke, severe pre-maturity of birth, and control of the prime risk factors for death, like hypertension and diabetes, are superior under medical care in the United States. Availability of state-of the-art medical technology, timely access to specialists, the most effective screening, the shortest wait times for life-changing surgeries, the newest most effective drugs for more accurate, safer diagnosis and for the most advanced treatment are all superior in the United States."

The main problem with the American health care system has been rapidly rising costs, which are increasing federal spending on health care, and the lack of access for many Americans. The number of people who do not have health insurance offers one measure of the lack of access, but the reported numbers do not take into account that many people who do not have insurance are already eligible for federal programs or are undocumented immigrants. Moreover, people without health insurance have some access to health care, while some people on government insurance programs like Medicaid have limited access because reimbursement rates are so low.

Good reforms to the American health care system can be found in the basic principles of economic freedom. First, remove restrictions on the types of health insurance firms can offer and people can buy—such as those that prevent people from buying health insurance in different states, or those that prevent or outlaw high deductibles or high copayments and thus lower-premium insurance plans; removing these restrictions will lower cost through competition and give Americans more choice. Second, reform federal health care programs as described in the next chapter by devolving Medicaid decisions to the states so that Americans with lower incomes have better access to better health care at lower costs and by giving more choice about Medicare insurance to senior citizens so they have the same kind of options they now have for prescription drugs. Third, level the playing field by providing the same tax-deductibility rules for health care to individuals that are now provided only to employers; this would "significantly reduce the growth in health costs," as explained in the book *Healthy, Wealthy, and Wise,* by John Cogan, Glenn Hubbard, and Daniel Kessler.

Step Back and Move Forward

Government regulation should rely more on the rule of law and less on the rule of men. Any plan to restore American prosperity must remove the regulatory drag on the economy and the crony capitalism and regulatory capture that magnify it. Consistent with principles of economic freedom and proposals in the two previous chapters, which would roll back recent excesses in fiscal and monetary policy, the 2010 financial legislation and the 2010 health care legislation should be scaled back or amended and replaced with legislation based on market incentives and the rule of law, not on the discretion of government bureaucracies.

To jump-start this reform agenda, a general moratorium

on new regulations should be enacted with exceptions for national security or public health and safety. To promote economic growth, all regulations should be transparent and simple. Transparency and simplicity will go a long way toward combating regulatory capture and preventing the mistakes that led to the financial crisis where the regulatory rules on the books were not enforced. Lack of enforcement of existing regulations was more of a problem than too few regulations.

New regulations should also pass rigorous cost-benefit tests. Estimates of the costs and the benefits of these regulations should be published before new regulations are put into law or promulgated by regulatory agencies. With enhanced public debate and clear legislative processes, we can arrive at regulatory laws appropriate for a properly working economy.

6

......

Improving Lives While Spiking the Entitlement Explosion

Entitlement reform has stalled in America for many reasons. A lack of reform proposals is not one of them. Budget experts—many working quietly at think tanks or for special government commissions—have proposed and analyzed hundreds of reform plans. The Congressional Budget Office (CBO) has pored over thirty different reform proposals for Social Security alone, and there are many more for the other two big entitlement programs, Medicaid and Medicare, and still more for entitlements that work through the tax system, such as child care or tuition tax credits. Each of these programs has already become quite complex, and the reform plans are even more complex, which makes them difficult for concerned citizens to evaluate and ripe for false partisan charges and attacks.

To kick-start a reform process, we should start with some basic facts and principles. An entitlement is a program in which the government makes automatic payments to people who pass certain eligibility criteria, usually related to age, income, or health status. Budget experts refer to entitlement spending as "automatic pilot" spending. Sometimes people warn about an "entitlement state" in which entitlement programs infiltrate a country's economy so thoroughly that they destroy economic freedom and threaten the very prosperity that made the entitlements possible in the first place. So where does America stand now and where is it going?

Cradle to Grave?

A large percentage of Americans now qualify for entitlement spending. According to the U.S. Census Bureau, about 55 percent of all American households receive an entitlement payment of some kind from the federal government. Examples include payments from Medicaid, the Earned Income Credit, Temporary Assistance to Needy Families (TANF), food stamps, housing subsidies, and school lunch programs, as well as the social insurance programs such as Social Security, Medicare, and unemployment compensation. This percentage understates federal support because the payments do not include many other subsidies such as research grants and agricultural support programs.

Of course, virtually 100 percent of households with a senior citizen receive entitlement payments from Social Security or Medicare, but even when we exclude retirees, about 41 percent of American households receive some form of entitlement payment.

For certain types of households without a senior citizen present, the percentage is much higher than for the population as a whole. About 80 percent of households headed by a single mother receive entitlement payments. More than half of American children now live in households receiving some federal entitlement benefits. Because they represent the future, the statistics on children are a leading indicator of where the already high penetration of the entitlement system in America is going.

The primary purpose of entitlement programs—a purpose quite consistent with the principles of economic freedom—is to help the needy and provide a social safety net to those who have fallen through the cracks. The question is whether the entitlement programs have grown, or are growing, so large that they go well beyond that purpose and instead create harmful disincentives or crisis-threatening pressures on the budget and federal finances.

The Coming Entitlement Explosion

How big are these entitlement programs? How rapidly are they growing? How do they compare to the size of the total federal budget or the size of the economy? Social Security spending is now about 21 percent of total federal spending. Federal health care programs—including Medicare for the elderly, Medicaid for people with low incomes, and the 2010 health care law, which expands access to health care and greatly increases entitlement payments—are now 24 percent of the budget. All these programs are expected to grow in the future, as the chart on the next page demonstrates.

The chart shows federal spending on Social Security and health care as a percentage of current GDP, as well as their projections into the future. The CBO made these projections assuming that the entitlement laws currently on the books remain in effect. Social Security is now about 5 percent of GDP and is projected to grow to about 6 percent of GDP over the next thirty years. The increase is partly due to the baby-boom generation's retirement, which has just begun, but also to rising payments per retiree even after adjusting for inflation.

Federal medical care entitlement spending is already about 6 percent of GDP, but it is expected to double to 12 percent of GDP over the next thirty years. The rapid growth is in part due to a projected increase in the number of retirees on Medicare, but also to the rising payments per retiree, which grow even faster than Social Security payments as medical costs rise. Summing the 12 percent of GDP for health care and the 6 percent of GDP for Social Security gives a total of 18 percent of GDP for these entitlements in thirty years, more than twice as large as the 8 percent of GDP for all other government spending—excluding interest payments—combined.

Federal Spending on Social Security and Health Care as a Percentage of GDP

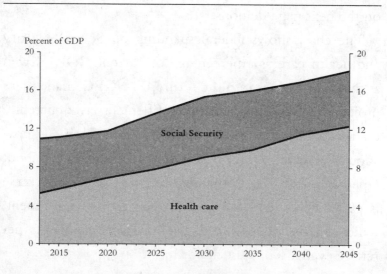

The growth in these programs provides the main fuel for the rapidly growing debt we saw in chapter 3. To defuse the debt explosion, we must first spike the entitlement spending explosion.

Harmful Disincentives

Another way to grasp the scope of the entitlements expansion is to examine how individuals are affected. Under the 2010 health care law, subsidy payments to buy health insurance are paid to households earning as much as 400 percent of the poverty line if they do not have insurance from an employer. With the poverty line equal to about $23,300 for a family of four, families earning $90,000 per year will be entitled to a payment. Such subsidies go well beyond reasonable definitions of a social safety net, and other families and individuals earning less than $90,000 will have to pay part of the tax bill to support this entitlement.

Entitlement programs also create powerful disincentive effects, especially when they get too big. The health care subsidy in the 2010 act declines as a family earns more income, and then is cut to zero when 400 percent of the poverty line is hit. This creates a situation where if you work more, you earn less. Consider a family earning $80,000 that gets a health care subsidy from the government of $16,100 under the 2010 health care law, bringing their total income to $96,100. Now suppose that the husband or the wife decides to work more. If they increase their income from work by $14,000, bringing their work earnings to $94,000, then their health care subsidy drops to zero. So they get less income by working more, and that's a big disincentive for the economy to grow. While the disincentives may not be as large in other cases, they will still discourage work to some degree.

In sum, whether measured by the share of GDP, by the share of the federal budget, by the impact on the debt, or by the effects on families and individuals, the growing size and scope of government entitlement programs cannot be considered limited by any reasonable definition of economic freedom. A reform consistent with the principles of economic freedom would stop the increase in entitlement spending as a share of GDP and at least hold it in place and make the spending more beneficial to people. Of course, with GDP growing, the dollar amounts spent on the programs would continue to grow under such a reform.

Medicare Reform: Two Ways to Spike the Explosion

Enacting these reforms will require making fundamental changes to our entitlement programs, especially those related to health care. The reforms must (1) place limits on spending growth and (2) change the programs to hold actual spending growth to these limits.

There are two major approaches to achieve these ends, and they are illustrated by two proposals for Medicare reform, one put forth by Congressman Paul Ryan on April 6, 2011, and the other by President Barack Obama on April 13, 2011. Ryan's plan transforms Medicare into a marketplace of decentralized, regulated, private-insurance policies in which each individual's Medicare entitlement consists of government-provided support to pay insurance premiums. The total amount of the premium support grows over time at a rate appropriate to limit the growth of the total cost of the program. Obama's plan retains Medicare's current structure, in which the government itself is the insurer making payments to doctors and hospitals, but with the overlay of a new, centralized bureaucracy to limit the growth of costs.

Both plans place limits on spending growth that are far below those projected under the current Medicare law. This is the most important thing to remember when considering the alternative plans. Both stop the projected explosion of Medicare spending. They flatten it out; spending as a share of GDP is much less than it would otherwise be in future years. But neither plan cuts spending in dollar terms or relative to current levels of spending.

To be sure there are small differences in the ways the plans set limits on spending growth. The Obama plan starts limiting spending growth earlier, in 2014, rather than in 2022 as in the Ryan plan. It caps Medicare spending per beneficiary at the rate of growth of GDP per capita plus ½ percent, while Ryan's plan caps spending per beneficiary at the growth in the consumer price index. As a result, the Obama Medicare spending growth rate is likely to be slightly lower than Ryan's in the near future and higher than the Ryan plan in later years. Given the urgent need to resolve our current fiscal predicament, the lower early limits in the Obama plan are an advantage.

Nevertheless, the two approaches are similar in that both appear to be guided by the goal of limiting the growth of Medicare spending compared to what is now projected. The difference between the approaches is found in how much they lean toward, or away from, the principles of economic freedom. The Ryan plan adheres particularly well to all five but especially to the rule of law, policy predictability, markets, and incentives. It is similar to the Medicare Part D prescription drug benefit plan, in which private insurance firms deliver the insurance policy chosen by the Medicare recipient. It encourages competition among private insurance plans and provides incentives for beneficiaries to make cost-conscious choices among plans. In contrast, the Obama plan would empower a new

Independent Payment Advisory Board (IPAB) to identify the drivers of excessive and unnecessary Medicare spending and recommend policies to Congress to curtail that spending.

Ryan's approach vests ultimate responsibility for cost containment with individuals and families, who spend within their means much more than the government. It commits the government to spending a specific dollar amount, rather than an amorphous promise to eliminate unnecessary care. Without a credible commitment to cost control, the incentives of doctors, hospitals, and patients will be to spend more and more.

For these reasons the Ryan plan would result in better health services for each Medicare dollar spent, because it uses market prices to allocate resources rather than the prices set by government bureaucrats. We already know that politically determined prices cause too much spending on some items and too little on others. For example, a study by researchers at the Medicare Payment Advisory Commission published in 2008 in *Health Affairs* found that Medicare's overpayment for imaging services contributed to rapid spending growth in the program.

The Ryan approach would better protect older beneficiaries and those with poor health or low incomes. Such protections are also the intent of the Obama plan, but that plan simply promises that the IPAB will not reduce access or quality of care. The Ryan plan explicitly gives older and sicker beneficiaries a larger premium support payment. Wealthier beneficiaries receive a smaller one.

Centralized, government-run insurance systems faced with resource constraints ration care by restricting eligibility for treatment. The London newspaper *The Independent* reported in July 2011 that cataract operations in Britain's National Health Service were being withheld until patients' sight problems "substantially" affect their ability to work. Hip and knee replacements are being allowed only when patients are in extreme pain.

As Medicare has reduced payment rates, doctors have begun requesting additional fees from Medicare beneficiaries, which has the effect of encouraging a two-tiered medical system. Although such "concierge" or "retainer" payments are still rare in some parts of the country, they have become more prevalent in Los Angeles, Miami, New York, and Washington.

For Medicare reform, the question is not whether to spike the spending explosion. Both Obama-type proposals and Ryan-type proposals do that. The question is how best to improve people's lives—promoting quality, protecting the poorest and sickest among us, preserving the program for future generations—while spiking the explosion. The keys once again are the principles of economic liberty, with more patient involvement and freedom to choose health care plans in a system that creates competitive market conditions for insurance companies and pharmaceutical firms.

Medicaid: States Know Better

The best way to reform Medicaid is to turn the program over to the states, with the federal government providing funding through block grants that grow at a pace consistent with controlling overall federal entitlement spending. This frees the states to design and choose the program that is most appropriate for people with low incomes in their state.

A similar "devolution" to the states occurred in 1996 when Congress passed and President Clinton signed the Personal Responsibility and Work Opportunity Reconciliation Act (PRWORA) of 1996, a law that was supposed to "end welfare as we know it" and did. The entitlement program Aid to Families with Dependent Children (AFDC) was transformed into another type of entitlement program, Temporary Assistance for Needy Families (TANF), with work and other requirements as each state saw fit within broad federal guidelines.

A marked reduction in welfare dependency and welfare caseloads resulted. Spending was down too. Real federal and state government spending on TANF in 2006 was

31 percent lower than government spending on AFDC in 1995. The welfare reform worked well because it recognized the states' economic freedom from the federal government and gave them the power to make their own decisions. The Medicaid program would undoubtedly see the same kind of improvement with this type of reform, as states would find ways to make the program more efficient, improve its quality, and increase access for Medicaid recipients.

One criticism of proposals to devolve Medicaid to the states maintains that the block grants from the federal government would not grow sufficiently to cover the increased medical costs over time. The Ryan plan for Medicare sometimes faces similar arguments, where critics claim that insufficient growth in premium supports would require recipients to make up the difference out of their own pockets. But as my comparison between the Ryan and Obama Medicare plans makes clear, the real issue is not whether we should stop the explosion of entitlement spending, but rather how we do it and at the same time improve people's lives. The comparison should be between a devolution approach and a centralized approach in which spending growth is the same in each case. For the reasons stressed throughout this chapter, and indeed throughout this book, the decentralized approach will work better because it more thoroughly reflects the principles of economic freedom.

Social Security

It is well known that as the baby-boom generation ages, a larger fraction of American households will be entitled to receive Social Security payments. The percentage of the population sixty-five and older, as a fraction of those between twenty and sixty-five, is now 22 percent. As the baby boomers age, the percentage will rise to 27 percent in 2020 and to 35 percent in 2030.

But what is less well known is that under current law, Social Security payments per retiree are rising in real terms even after adjusting for inflation, in the sense that higher benefits are to be paid to future retirees than to today's retirees. A forty-five-year-old today is scheduled to get an inflation-adjusted initial retirement benefit that is 40 percent higher than the benefit for a typical current retiree. A thirty-five-year-old is scheduled to get 55 percent more than current retirees. A twenty-five-year-old is scheduled to get 71 percent more. A reasonable reform would simply keep benefits for future retirees at the same level, adjusted for inflation, as today's retirees. This would hold Social Security spending to about the same share of

GDP that it takes up today, helping to spike the spending explosion and make Social Security sustainable without increasing tax rates.

To understand how this reform would work, we need to know how the government calculates Social Security payments under current law. First, the government finds a person's average earnings over his or her top thirty-five earnings years, adjusting upward the earnings in the early years by the rate of wage increase in the overall economy during those years. This average is called the average indexed monthly earnings (AIME). The government then determines the initial benefit, called the primary insurance amount (PIA), by taking 90 percent of the first $761 of AIME, plus 32 percent of the next $3,825, plus 15 percent of the remaining. Thus, people with higher average earnings over their lifetime get a smaller percentage in benefits than people with lower lifetime earnings. This introduces progressivity into Social Security. These percentages are called the "PIA factors." The dollar amounts at which the PIA factors initially apply—for example, amounts at which the 90 percent goes to 32 percent, and the 32 percent goes to 15 percent—are adjusted up over time according to the amount of wage inflation in the economy. Finally, the initial benefit is adjusted over time during retirement at the rate of inflation.

A Golden Rule Reform

A simple reform that achieves the goal of keeping initial benefits for future generations roughly the same as initial benefits for current generations would be to adjust PIA factors down in the future if wages grow more rapidly than prices. This reform is actually one of the thirty that the CBO has analyzed. In the CBO version, the reform would start in 2017. Effectively, initial benefits would increase with prices rather than with wages. The amounts would thus be contingent on real wage growth, or the growth of wages over and above prices. If wage growth declined relative to price growth, then the adjustment would be smaller; if wage growth increased relative to price growth, then the adjustment would be larger.

An advantage of this proposal is that the percentage changes from the current law would be exactly the same for every person in a birth cohort. Thus everyone within a birth cohort is contributing the same percentage share to the reform. The income distribution is not affected. The progressivity of Social Security payments remains the same. Another advantage is that average real benefits would be maintained over time.

Some will argue that although maintaining the average real initial benefit over time is appealing, the dollar amount of the initial benefit will be lower relative to wage earnings, because as labor productivity improves, wages grow over time somewhat faster than prices. In fact, the CBO estimates that initial benefits as a fraction of AIME would decline from 44 percent to 29 percent as benefits are maintained in terms of purchasing power.

Under the proposal, benefits will continue to grow at the rate of inflation, but they do not grow faster than the rate of inflation as in the current law. The forty-five-year-old today will not be getting 40 percent more than a person who retires this year, but rather about the same amount adjusted for inflation. In terms of purchasing power of the benefits to buy goods and services, it thus provides the same safety net to each generation of seniors who have little or no other income.

Such a plan also offer advantages compared to other reform plans. For example, another proposal to reduce the growth of benefits would increase the retirement age more rapidly. But that plan will adversely affect people with labor-intensive jobs in construction, mining, and other industries for whom a delayed retirement and more years on the job is a very difficult if not impossible prospect. At the same time, however, "Americans who wish to work for more than forty years, into their sixties, seventies, or eighties, should not be penalized with high tax rates," which currently reach 85 percent, as George

Shultz and John Shoven argue in their book *Putting Our House in Order.*

There are variants on the golden rule proposal. One could twist the PIA factors to favor people with lower incomes, by reducing the PIA factor at the top part of the wage earnings distribution by more in percentage terms than the factors at the lower part of the distribution. In this way future benefits would decline in real terms for people with higher lifetime incomes and rise in real terms for people with lower lifetime incomes.

This reform plan for Social Security shares the spirit of the Medicare reform plans put forth by President Obama and Congressman Ryan. Those plans endeavor to keep entitlement spending from rising too much as a share of GDP. The same is true for this Social Security reform plan. Over the next thirty years, total outlays would decline as a share of GDP by about 1 percentage point compared with current law, which would exactly offset the currently projected increase of 1 percent of GDP. In addition, Social Security would be sustainable in the long run without any increase in Social Security taxes on payrolls.

Why Aren't Revenues on the Table?

The entitlement reform proposals described in this chapter crucially do not entail an increase in tax rates. Neither the Social Security payroll tax of 12.4 percent of wages (shared 50-50 by employees and employers) up to an annual wage maximum ($106,800 in 2011) nor the 2.9 percent Medicare tax (also shared 50-50) on all wages is increased. In comparison, many other entitlement reform proposals, including some of those analyzed by the CBO, require tax increases.

There are four reasons why tax increases are not part of my proposals. First, higher tax rates would further reduce incentives to work or hire or expand and are inadvisable as a policy to restore economic growth, especially in a slow recovery period. Second, spending is the primary culprit in the deficit and debt problem. To defuse the debt explosion with tax increases rather than reductions in spending growth would require tax rates of an untenable 75 percent or more. We have to focus on spending. Third, the reform proposals purposely do not expand the entitlement state. For the reasons given in this chapter, further growth of entitlements would be detrimental per se. It would be a mistake to raise tax rates to fund an expansion of entitlements. Fourth, if we wish to affect the progressivity of entitlements, rather than raising taxes we could adjust the entitlements themselves by, for example, adjusting the Social Security system to tilt the benefits away from higher-income groups.

Some argue that we need to increase tax rates because

the income distribution has widened as the earnings of people in upper-income groups have grown faster than the earnings of those in lower-income groups. But this trend implies that we should reduce the amount of entitlements going to upper- or upper-middle-income groups and provide a better safety net for those at the bottom; it does not imply that we should raise tax rates. Indeed, a more rapid growth of incomes *before taxes* in upper-income groups drives most of the widening of the income distribution. Changes in tax rates have relatively little to do with it, as recent research by the CBO shows. The widening income distribution is caused in part by the tendency of our increasingly high-tech economy to give even greater rewards to higher-skilled workers and thereby increase the economic returns to education. The way to address the issue is to improve the quality of education. Indeed, education reform is another area that would benefit from greater attention to the principles of economic freedom.

This is not to say that tax reform is not necessary. As I explained in chapter 3, tax reform is an essential part of a pro-growth strategy. Indeed, tax reform, entitlement reform, regulatory reform, monetary reform, and budget reform should all be part of an economic plan to raise economic growth and make America a better place. In the next chapter we will see how the strategy will also make the world a better place.

7

Rebuilding American Economic Leadership

O ur abandonment of the principles of economic freedom has consequences at home and abroad. America's economic leadership on the world stage is under threat, and recent government policy has succeeded only in making us more vulnerable. It's a vulnerability the rest of the world sees. When Treasury Secretary Timothy Geithner went to China in June 2009, college students laughed out loud when he insisted in a speech that the dollar was strong and Chinese assets in America were safe. Indeed, the real purpose of his trip was to negotiate with the leaders of the Chinese government—America's largest creditor—and argue for a weaker dollar against their currency.

A year later, in June 2010, when Secretary Geithner met with the finance ministers of the world's twenty largest developed and emerging-market economies, the G20, they rejected his pleas for more deficit-increasing Keynesian stimulus and recommended exactly the opposite: credible budget deficit reduction. When President Obama met with his counterparts in the G20 a few months later, he was forced to defend America's central bank against widespread criticism of its activist interventions and the harm they were causing emerging-market economies.

In the meantime, many of those emerging-market economies had been steadily moving toward, rather than away from, the principles of economic freedom. Their economies had improved as a result. Brazil, India, Mexico, Turkey, and South Africa withstood the shock of the financial crisis better than anyone could have imagined given their crisis experiences in the 1990s. Each country's economic growth was strong, and ironically they were espousing the principles the United States had advocated in earlier years when American economic leadership was indisputable.

If this decline in American economic leadership continues, the rest of the world, which has benefited from America's promotion of economic freedom for decades, may suffer. Especially at a time of great upheaval—revolutions in information technology, tectonic demographic transitions, political awakenings in the Middle East and North Africa, a Chinese economy destined to be the largest in the world—America's first principles of economic freedom are more sorely needed than ever.

American Economic Leadership following World War II

In the years after the Great Depression and World War II, America was a beacon of democracy delivering a powerful message about what freedom, both economic and personal, could achieve. Yes, it used direct material assistance and voices over the airwaves to convey this message. But America's most effective argument was the country itself: its vibrant culture in the arts and entertainment, its contributions to the sciences, and its innovations in medical technology and pharmaceuticals, all underpinned by a prosperous economy copied first by Germany and Japan and later by China and the other high-growth emerging economies.

In the postwar period America created a rules-based open trading system that established the foundations of the global market economy. U.S. officials were instrumental in founding the multilateral General Agreement on Tar-

iffs and Trade in 1947, which set the stage for an economic boom through the wholesale removal of barriers
to buying and selling goods and services across borders.
The main American goal in founding the International
Monetary Fund in 1944 was to prevent debilitating
manipulations of exchange rates and remove restrictions
on making loans or selling securities to people in different countries. And America's initial goal in creating the
World Bank, also in 1944, was the reconstruction of market economies, first in Europe and later in the developing
world. The economic miracles that were the German and
Japanese recoveries owed much to the American model of
economic freedom and the direct support and encourage-
ment of the United States.

Falling Away

Unfortunately, American economic policy went off track
in the 1960s and 1970s, as we saw in chapter 1, with a
host of fiscal and monetary actions and interventions that
generated inflation, low productivity growth, and high
unemployment, and eventually led to further restrictions
on economic freedom, including price and wage controls.
The policy change had international ramifications and
affected America's global leadership.

In 1963 the U.S. government imposed a new international tax—the Interest Equalization Tax—on purchases of stocks and bonds abroad, hoping to shift purchases to the United States and thus prop up the demand for dollars. Operation Twist—in which the Federal Reserve bought long-term bonds and sold short-term bonds—sought to lower long-term interest rates to stimulate the economy without lowering short-term rates on dollar assets, which would have reduced the attractiveness of the dollar.

Europeans complained that the United States was exporting inflation with its expansionary monetary and fiscal policies, and it was. The downward pressure on the dollar caused by the inflation in the United States eventually led to the collapse in the early 1970s of the fixed exchange rate system that had been established in the Bretton Woods agreement after World War II. While these events raised questions about U.S. economic leadership, America was still instrumental in the post–Bretton Woods reform of the international financial system, establishing a more flexible exchange rate system within which different countries could choose monetary and fiscal policies better suited to their own circumstances.

Economic Freedom Returns and Spreads

By the early 1980s, America had begun to reassert its economic leadership. It got its own house in order. It stopped making short-term fiscal and monetary interventions. It permanently cut marginal tax rates. It reduced regulations. It relinquished some federal government power to the states. These pro-growth policies drove another economic boom that lasted through the 1990s. The inflation rate came down, and productivity growth went up. This return to the ideas of economic freedom was contagious, and other countries made similar policy changes. In Britain, Margaret Thatcher, followed by John Major and then Tony Blair, led the charge toward economic freedom.

The most dramatic change in this new era began in the developing world as the advantages of American-style economic liberty over state intervention and control became more and more clear. In China, Deng Xiaoping initiated market-based reforms and created an economic miracle that lifted millions from poverty and is still a wonderful sight to see. By the end of the 1980s, the Soviet Union's communist model was collapsing, with markets starting to replace government controls. In addition to serving as a role model, the United States directly helped the countries of Central and Eastern Europe to implement market-based reforms and encouraged other countries and the international financial institutions to do the same. Milton Friedman's 1962 book *Capitalism and Freedom*, which we now know had become an underground classic in these countries in the decade after it was written, was the openly cited bible of the reformers.

Poland offers a wonderful illustration of the reform movement. After Lech Walesa and the Solidarity trade-union movement triumphed politically over the communists, the new Polish government quickly developed economic-renewal plans that were ready to go by December 1989. These changes were sometimes called "shock therapy" because they were enacted so rapidly, or the Balcerowicz Plan, because Finance Minister Leszek Balcerowicz supported them more than anyone else in the Polish government.

The plan quickly transformed the economy by removing many price controls and halting subsidies to state enterprises. The United States was a strong advocate of the plan. As a member of President George H. W. Bush's Council of Economic Advisers, I worked with Condoleezza Rice, who was then the National Security Council's director of Soviet and Eastern European affairs, to put together a $1 billion stabilization plan to help the transition and demonstrate American support.

At first Poland's economic transformation was very difficult. The state enterprises, suddenly left to compete in the free market without price supports and subsidies, were exposed as unprofitable. Many had to close or shrink. Unemployment rose. I traveled to Warsaw in December

1989, and again in April 1990, to provide advice. On the second visit the team included former Federal Reserve chairman Paul Volcker. I recall the distressed prime minister of Poland, Tadeusz Mazowiecki, asking us in a small meeting if we could see "light at the end of the tunnel" for the Polish people. Volcker, who had experience with America's painful disinflation in the early 1980s, offered strong support and said that Poland should stick to the plan. Almost everyone in the group of advisers agreed. Fortunately, Poland emerged successfully from the transition. Its new economy started recovering and was growing again by 1992, and it remains relatively strong today. Poland was the only nation in Europe to avoid a recession after the 2008 financial turmoil.

By the early years of the twenty-first century, Brazil under President Lula, Turkey under Prime Minister Erdoğan, and many other emerging-market countries were moving to sounder monetary and fiscal policies and growing faster, with fewer crises. Bailouts of emerging-market countries and their creditors by the International Monetary Fund stopped as the fund put in place more predictable limits on bailouts to emerging-market countries.

The United States provided material assistance in some cases of economic transformation. After the ouster of Saddam Hussein from Iraq, it lent its skills and provided funds to create a workable market economy and financial system in Iraq to go along with democratic reforms. It signed free-trade agreements with countries in the Middle East—Bahrain, Morocco, and Oman—and created in 2004 the Broader Middle East and North Africa Initiative to explore more economic engagement and encourage economic reforms.

Leading from Behind?

Unfortunately, in the past few years the United States has shifted away from its promotion of economic freedom around the world. Congressional action on U.S. trade agreements that had been negotiated before 2009, such as with Colombia and South Korea, was delayed by the Obama administration for three years for seemingly inexplicable reasons. Only one free-trade agreement, the Trans Pacific Partnership Agreement, has been initiated for negotiations since 2009.

The U.S. government has also been promoting short-term Keynesian policies around the world, in 2010 and 2011, long after the panic in the fall of 2008, and it has been unable to persuade other governments to go along. A letter from Treasury Secretary Geithner to his G20 colleagues released just before their June 2010 meeting was packed with calls for governments to pursue fiscal stimulus in order to generate more aggregate demand. But at that meeting, the G20 finance ministers and central-bank governors produced a stark rejection of American calls for more fiscal stimulus. Nowhere in the official G20 communiqué did the ministers and governors call on each other to stimulate aggregate demand with more expansionary fiscal policy. Instead, they said things like "We welcome the recent announcements by some countries to reduce their deficits in 2010 and strengthen their fiscal frameworks and institutions." You do not have to be an insider to know that this was a rejection of U.S. leadership. The word "demand" had appeared eight times in Geithner's June letter, but not once in the final G20 statement. His G20 counterparts saw that too much government borrowing caused their problems rather than solved them. They had learned from experience that debt-increasing stimulus packages did more harm than good. When in September 2011 the Obama administration proposed yet-another deficit-increasing, short-term Keynesian stimulus, the G20 instead called at its next meeting for countries to "implement clear, credible and specific measures to achieve fiscal consolidation."

That same September, Treasury Secretary Geithner traveled to Europe specifically for the purpose of recommending very large bailouts and large bailout funds— championing the same flawed mindset that had seized the U.S. government in the lead-up to the American financial crisis. The reaction has not been good for the United States. When German Finance Minister Wolfgang Schäuble heard the recommendation, he broke all diplomatic decorum and said that the ideas were "stupid."

In the political upheaval now occurring in the Middle East and North Africa (MENA), the United States and its Western allies are downplaying economic freedom instead of championing it as they did in post-communist Eastern Europe. America could do more to promote economic freedom in the newly free countries of the Middle East and North Africa, first by strongly supporting economic leaders who are committed to creating a private market economy.

It is alarming to hear that international support packages for Tunisia and Egypt may do just the opposite: encourage more government subsidies and controls. The young entrepreneur who immolated himself in Tunisia and started the Jasmine Revolution was simply trying to open and run a small business in a country with little economic freedom. Yet in a letter to President Obama, French President Sarkozy, and other world leaders meeting in France in 2011, a group of well-known economists—most from Europe but including America-based Keynesian economists Joseph Stiglitz and Nouriel Roubini—started with the case for government subsidies. Instead, Tunisia needs to reduce barriers to entrepreneurship and job creation. It needs to open its economy domestically and internationally. It needs to adopt the principles of economic freedom. And it needs the support of the United States as it does so.

Are there new leaders in the Arab world who will support such economic changes? Of course there are. The new Tunisian central bank governor, Mustapha Nabli, who obtained a Ph.D. in economics from UCLA in 1974, wrote in a book, *Breaking the Barriers to Higher Economic Growth: Better Governance and Deeper Reforms in the Middle East and North Africa*, that "at its core, [economic growth] requires the region's public sector-dominated economies to move to private sector-driven economies, from closed economies to more open economies, and from oil-dominated and volatile economies to more stable and diversified economies." He based his case on hard facts, including a careful empirical comparison of Eastern European transitions with those occurring in the Middle East and North Africa, and an analysis of reform in practice that strongly suggests a serious, relatively fast-paced reform worthy of America's support.

What Goes Around Comes Around

Deviations from economic freedom in America affect the rest of the world in often subtle ways, especially in the important case of monetary policy, but if we look at policy decisions among countries active in global financial markets, one effect becomes quite clear.

Interest rate decisions by central banks, most significantly the interest rate set by the Fed, tend to influence interest rate decisions at other central banks. If the Fed holds its interest rate too low for too long, then central banks in other countries will tend to do the same. If a central bank resisted this tendency and kept its interest rate up when U.S. interest rates were cut to very low levels, investors in search of better yields would rush into the country's currency. The investment influx would drive up the value of the currency, making exports from the country very expensive abroad and shifting the demand for exports down. Falling demand would in turn produce a sharp decline in exports, which could adversely affect the economy. At the very least, the drop would draw criticism from the country's exporters, who are often powerful political forces in open economies where international trade is the lifeblood.

Most central banks are not transparent enough to reveal this interest rate sensitivity directly, but it becomes quite clear in more transparent ones such as Norges Bank and Riksbank, the central banks of Norway and Sweden, respectively. Consider the policy discussion at the Riksbank in September 2010. The publically released records of that discussion reveal concern about the interest rates set by central banks in the larger economies. At the time, Deputy Governor Lars Svensson preferred to hold the Swedish interest rate very low for a period of time while others wanted to increase the rate sooner, or by a larger amount. Their debate focused on what other central banks, in particular the Fed and the European Central Bank, would do. As the record of the meeting put it, continuance of very low interest rates in the United States "must be regarded as very realistic." Although the interest rate should be higher given internal conditions in Sweden, with such a higher interest rate the "differential in relation to other countries would be considerable. This would trigger substantial capital flows and lead to a dramatic appreciation of the krona." As a result of such considerations, the rate was held relatively low. The stated rationales for decisions at Norges Bank reveal the same tendency. With most other central banks, which are less transparent, to detect the reasons for their moves we have to examine the available data and use statistical methods, but the tendency to act as the Swedes and Norwegians did is much the same.

This interaction among central banks caused global short-term interest rates to be lower than they otherwise would have been in the period from 2003 to 2005, when the Fed held its interest rate too low. In fact, it appears that a good portion of the European Central Bank's interest rate moves during this time can be explained by the influence of the Fed's interest rate decisions. There is only one euro interest rate in the Eurozone, which consists of the countries that use the euro as their currency, including Greece, Germany, France, Spain, Italy, and Ireland among others. The European Central Bank has responsibility for setting an interest rate, which then applies to all the countries in the Eurozone. By my estimates, the interest rate set by the European Central Bank was as much as two percentage points too low during the 2003–2005 period, and this deviation may largely be attributed to the Federal Reserve.

We've already reviewed the damage done by low rates to the U.S. economy, but how harmful were the low rates in Europe? In a study published in 2008, economists at the Organisation for Economic Co-operation and Development found that low rates were the cause of the housing booms in Greece, Ireland, and Spain, where housing construction was 3 to 6 percentage points higher as a share of GDP than it otherwise would have been. As with all unsustainable booms, these were rife with excessive risk-taking and were inevitably followed by busts; bad loan problems at banks led to huge government borrowing to bail out the banks or to finance spending when revenues fell during the recession. Thus, the low interest rate set for the Eurozone did considerable damage in the economies with booming housing markets and little damage in Germany and Austria, where the interest rates were about right for their economies. For Europe as a whole, a higher interest rate could have prevented the problems in Greece, Ireland, and Spain with little or no adverse consequences for other parts of the Eurozone.

Decisions by the American authorities to deviate from the rule-like behavior that worked so well during the 1980s and 1990s not only caused serious economic problems in the United States, but likely caused serious problems in Europe too. The European debt crisis, which originated in the booms and busts in Greece, Ireland, and Spain, has U.S. fingerprints on it. That debt crisis could, of course, come back to the original source of the disturbance, for example, if Europe's demand for U.S. exports drops as a result of its crisis.

The Fed has responded to the weak U.S. recovery with more interventions—from quantitative easing to a new Operation Twist—and a zero interest rate, with Ben Bernanke announcing in the summer of 2011 that he would try to hold the rate at zero for another two years. As we've seen, these policies make it harder for other central banks to raise interest rates and combat rising inflation in their countries without also creating damagingly large appreciations of their currencies. Most emerging-market central banks have felt the pressure. Some countries, including Brazil and China, have complained that the United States is exporting inflation, much like the European countries complained in the 1970s. To prevent currency appreciation, some have resorted to imposing restrictions on their companies' overseas borrowing or on foreigners investing in their countries.

Current American policy risks creating a rise in global inflation; in fact, it had already started to rise in most emerging markets in 2011. If inflation continues to rise or becomes ingrained, the higher prices abroad could easily feed back into higher prices and more inflation in the United States. With unemployment already high in the United States, the result would be a return to the stagflation of the 1970s. Once again, deviations from the principles of economic freedom are causing harm abroad and may come back to harm the United States. For the good of the world and thereby for its own good, America needs to show some economic leadership and better adhere to the principles of economic freedom.

China and the Future of Economic Freedom

There is no place where the principles of economic freedom are more important for future generations than in America's engagement with China. China's exchange rate policy has attracted the most political attention over the past decade. The international division at the U.S. Treasury, which I ran for four-plus years, has consistently invested time and diplomatic effort into persuading the Chinese to move toward a more flexible exchange rate, and in 2005 China finally did abandon its policy of pegging the exchange rate to the dollar. Since then the Chinese exchange rate has appreciated 30 percent against the dollar—moving from 8.3 yuan per dollar to 6.4 yuan per dollar—and it will likely appreciate more as the Chinese central bank raises its interest rate to combat inflation and the yuan thus becomes more attractive to investors.

A more serious problem remains: despite the introduction and enormous success of Deng Xiaoping's market reforms, the Chinese economic system still fails to embrace many of the principles of economic freedom. While it certainly has relied on markets and incentives, China has a weak rule of law and imposes barriers to trade. These issues are obvious to any American firm trying to do business within China, but as is often the case with violations of economic freedom, they spill over into violations of political freedom, as people are wary of speaking out for fear of retribution.

Particular instances of departure from the basic principles of economic freedom in China may seem small, but the effects can be large. Consider Wal-Mart, which operates 350 stores selling $7.5 billion worth of merchandise to the Chinese people. In October 2011 the Chinese government shut down thirteen stores and put Wal-Mart employees in jail for mistakenly labeling "nonorganic" pork as "organic" pork. The government rationale for the intervention was not clear as there was no safety issue. Perhaps, as conjectured by the *Wall Street Journal*'s John Bussey, the harsh punishment was designed as a lesson to other American stores or businesses in China. There are also government procurement rules that favor some firms over others, crony-capitalism style. Other laws require foreign firms to enter joint ventures with government-owned firms if they want to do business in China. They thereby transfer technology and know-how to China that can be used to compete against them in other markets

The U.S. government should be working to prevent such restrictions and more generally to promote the principles of economic freedom. But if America itself does not adhere to the principles, the argument will take the form of "Do as I say, not as I do." Indeed, if the United States continues to depart from sound fiscal principles, it will have less and less intellectual influence abroad. But more ominously, if it continues its borrowing binge, it will only become more indebted to China and other countries less committed to the principles of economic freedom.

What Can Be Done?

As with so much of this book, this chapter is a story of what *may* be, not what *will* be. And yet what may be reminds us of what is at stake. A decline in American economic leadership would be dangerous for the world economy and thus for America itself. An America transformed from a private sector–centered, producer-consumer nation to a government-administered social service provider would no longer be the "exceptional country" it was when it was founded. Nor would it remain the potent symbol of economic and political freedom it has been since its founding.

But if we refocus on the five key principles of economic freedom, elect leaders who are fully committed to these principles, who can implement them in practice, and who are confident enough to promote the principles abroad, we will avoid what may be. We will restore America's prosperity, benefit the world economy, and in turn lock a more prosperous American economy into a grand virtuous circle.

Notes

Preface

10–12 antecedents: Taylor, John B., *Global Financial Warriors: The Untold Story of International Finance in the Post-9/11 World*, New York, W. W. Norton, 2007; Taylor, John B., *Getting Off Track: How Government Actions and Interventions Caused, Prolonged, and Worsened the Financial Crisis*, Stanford, Calif., Hoover Institution Press, 2009.

12 shoulders of economic giants: Friedman, Milton, *Capitalism and Freedom*, Chicago, University of Chicago Press, 1962; *Economic Report of the President*, Washington, D.C., Government Printing Office, 1962. Since Walter Heller, James Tobin, and Kermit Gordon were the three original members of the Council of Economic Advisers, they had primary responsibility for writing this report, but other distinguished economists also served on the staff, including Arthur Okun and Robert Solow.

12 **Shultz quote:** Shultz, George P., "Reflections on Political Economy," *Challenge*, vol. 17, no. 1, 1975, p. 11 (published version of address before the Joint Meeting of the American Economic Association and the American Finance Association, December 28, 1973).

Chapter 1: First Principles Work

19 **textbook reference:** Taylor, John B., and Akila Weerapana, *Principles of Economics*, 7th ed., Mason, Ohio, South-Western Cengage Learning, 2012.

20 **Smith quote:** Smith, Adam, *An Inquiry into the Nature and Causes of the Wealth of Nations* [1776], New York, Random House, Modern Library Edition, 1994, p. 485.

22 **Hayek quote:** Hayek, F. A., *The Road to Serfdom* [1944], in Bruce Caldwell (ed.), *Collected Works of F. A. Hayek*, vol. 2, Chicago, University of Chicago Press, 2007, p. 112.

22 **Friedman quote:** Friedman, Milton, *Capitalism and Freedom*, Chicago, University of Chicago Press, 1962, p. 51.

30 **Friedman quote:** Friedman, Milton, "The Role of Monetary Policy," *American Economic Review*, vol. 58, no. 1, 1968.

31–32 **Eichenbaum quote:** Eichenbaum, Martin, "Some Thoughts on Practical Stabilization Policy," *American Economic Review*, vol. 87, no. 2, 1997, p. 17.

32 **Volcker quote:** Volcker, Paul A., "We Can Survive Prosperity," remarks at the Joint Meeting of the American Economic Association and the American Finance Association, December 28, 1983.

33 **Poole evidence of rules-based monetary policy in 1980s and 1990s:** Poole, William, "The Fed's Monetary Policy Rule," *Federal Reserve Bank of St. Louis Review*, January/February 2007.

33 **Judd-Trehan evidence of shift to rules-based monetary policy:** Judd, John P., and Bharat Trehan, "Has the Fed Gotten Tougher on Inflation?" *FRBSF Weekly Letter*, March 31, 1995.

34 **Friedman quote:** Pine, Art, "Friedman Boos, Stiglitz Cheers and Keynes Returns to Washington," *Bloomberg News*, October 18, 2001.

36 **author's testimony:** Taylor, John B., "The State of the Economy and Principles for Fiscal Stimulus," testimony before the Committee on the Budget, United States Senate, Washington, D.C., November 19, 2008.

37 **index of economic freedom:** Miller, Terry, and Kim R. Holmes, *2011 Index of Economic Freedom*, Washington, D.C., Heritage Foundation, 2011.

44 **Blinder on tax rebates:** Blinder, Alan S., "Temporary Income Taxes and Consumer Spending," *Journal of Political Economy*, vol. 89, no. 1, 1981.

44 **Blinder quote on price controls:** Blinder, Alan S., and William J. Newton, "The 1971–1974 Controls Program and the Price Level: An Econometric Post-Mortem," *Journal of Monetary Economics*, vol. 8, no. 1, 1981.

44 **author's evidence on impact of low interest rates:** Taylor, John B., "Housing and Monetary Policy," in *Housing, Housing Finance, and Monetary Policy*, Federal Reserve Bank of Kansas City, September 2007.

44 **Kahn on cause of housing bubble:** Kahn, George A., "Taylor Rule Deviations and Financial Imbalances," *Federal Reserve Bank of Kansas City Economic Review*, second quarter, 2010.

44–45 **author's evidence on 2001, 2008, 2009 stimulus packages:** Taylor, John B., "An Empirical Analysis of the Revival of Fiscal Activism in the 2000s," *Journal of Economic Literature*, vol. 49, no. 3, 2011.

45 Cogan-Taylor evidence on impact of stimulus grants: Cogan, John F., and John B. Taylor, "Where Did the Stimulus Go?" *Commentary*, January 2011.

45 Evidence on QE1: Stroebel, Johannes C., and John B. Taylor, "Estimated Impact of the Fed's Mortgage-Backed Securities Purchase Program," *International Journal of Central Banking*, in press (2012).

47 books on the Great Depression: Friedman, Milton, and Anna J. Schwartz, *A Monetary History of the United States: 1876–1960*, Princeton, N.J., Princeton University Press, 1963; Meltzer, Allan H., *A History of the Federal Reserve, Volume 1: 1913–1951*, Chicago, University of Chicago Press, 2003. Shlaes, Amity, *The Forgotten Man: A New History of the Great Depression*, New York, HarperCollins, 2007.

47 quote about Hoover: Shlaes, Amity, *The Forgotten Man: A New History of the Great Depression*, New York, HarperCollins, 2007, p. 34.

48 Cole-Ohanian quote: Cole, Harold L., and Lee E. Ohanian, "How Government Prolonged the Depression," *Wall Street Journal*, February 2, 2009.

Chapter 2: Who Gets Us In and Out of These Messes?

53 quote on tax reduction: *Economic Report of the President*, Washington, D.C.: Government Printing Office, 1977, p. 26.

54 quote on temporary tax rebates: Ibid.

55 quote from Greenspan memo to Ford: Mieczkowski, Yanek, *Gerald Ford and the Challenges of the 1970s*, Lexington, University of Kentucky Press, 2005, p. 169.

57 Schultze quote before House Committee on the Budget: Biven, W. Carl, *Jimmy Carter's Economy: Policy in* *an Age of Limits*, Chapel Hill, University of North Carolina Press, 2001, p. 70.

58 **Sunley quote:** Sunley, Emil M., "A Tax Preference Is Born: A Legislative History of the New Jobs Tax Credit," in Henry J. Aaron and Michael J. Boskin (eds.), *The Economics of Taxation*, Washington, D.C., Brookings Institution, 1980, p. 408.

58 **Gramlich quote:** Gramlich, Edward M., "Stimulating the Macro Economy through State and Local Governments," *American Economic Review*, vol. 69, no. 2, 1979, p. 180.

60 **Samuelson quote:** Interview with Nathan Gardels, "Don't Expect Recovery before 2012—With 8% Inflation," *New Perspectives Quarterly*, vol. 16, no. 1, 2009.

61 **quotes on discretionary policy:** *Economic Report of the President*, Washington, D.C., Government Printing Office, 1962, pp. 71, 72, 85.

63 **Friedman quote:** Friedman, Milton, and Walter Heller, *Monetary vs. Fiscal Policy: A Dialogue*, New York, W. W. Norton, 1969, p. 48.

65–66 **Martin quote:** Meltzer, Allan H., *A History of the Federal Reserve, Volume 2, Book 1*, Chicago, University of Chicago Press, 2009, p. 85.

66 **Meltzer quote:** Ibid., p. 485.

68 **Friedman 1971 column:** Friedman, Milton, "Steady as You Go," *Newsweek*, July 26, 1971.

68 **Shultz 1971 speech:** Shultz, George P., "Prescription for Economic Policy: 'Steady as You Go,'" address before the Economic Club of Chicago, April 22, 1971.

69 **Friedman 1973 column:** Friedman, Milton, "'Steady as You Go' Revisited," *Newsweek*, May 14, 1973.

70 **Shultz quote about lost battle:** George P. Shultz, letter to the author, January 3, 2011.

Notes

70 **Shultz quote about Connally:** Conversation with the author.

70 **Shultz quote about lags and nightmares**: Conversation with the author.

71 **McCracken quote and Roosevelt Room story:** Jones, Sidney L., *Public and Private Economic Adviser: Paul W. McCracken*, Lanham, Md., University Press of America, 2000, p. 280.

72 **Burns quote:** Burns, Arthur F., "The Problem of Inflation," address before the Joint Meeting of the American Economic Association and the American Finance Association, December 29, 1972.

72 **Ford quote:** Rumsfeld, Donald, *Known and Unknown: A Memoir*, New York, Sentinel, Penguin Group, 2011, p. 183.

72–73 **Ford quote on Whip Inflation Now:** Ford, Gerald R., "Address to a Joint Session of Congress on the Economy," Washington, D.C., October 8, 1974.

72–74 **Meltzer quote on different ideas from Nixon advisers:** Meltzer, Allan H., *A History of the Federal Reserve, Volume 2, Book 1*, Chicago, University of Chicago Press, 2009, pp. 485–486.

74–75 **Reagan's writings before his presidency:** Skinner, Kiron K., Annelise Anderson, and Martin Anderson, *Reagan in His Own Hand: The Writings of Ronald Reagan That Reveal His Revolutionary Vision for America*, New York, Free Press, 2001.

76 **Anderson quote:** Anderson, Martin, *Revolution*, New York, Harcourt Brace Jovanovich, 1988, p. 264.

77 **economic advisor memo:** "Economic Strategy for the Reagan Administration: A Report to President-Elect Ronald Reagan from His Coordinating Committee on Economic Policy," November 16, 1980.

Notes

80 **Volcker quote on** *Face the Nation*: Meltzer, Allan H., *A History of the Federal Reserve, Volume 2, Book 2*, Chicago, University of Chicago Press, 2009, p. 1023.

82–83 **quotes on benefits of systematic policy:** *Economic Report of the President*, Washington, D.C., Government Printing Office, 1990, pp. 84, 86.

83 **article about 1990 report:** Wessel, David, "A Bush Economist Is Urging Hands Off," *Wall Street Journal*, March 12, 1990.

84 **Clinton quotes on big government and welfare reform:** Clinton, William Jefferson, "State of the Union Address," Washington, D.C., January 23, 1996.

86 **O'Neill quote on tax rebate:** Suskind, Ron, *The Price of Loyalty*, New York, Simon and Schuster, 2004, p. 137.

87 **Bush quote on temporary tax cut:** Roth, Bennett, and David Ivanovich, "Bush Says Tax Cut Is Still Vital to Economy," *Houston Chronicle*, March 28, 2001.

88–89 **Friedman quote:** Friedman, Milton, and Walter Heller, *Monetary vs. Fiscal Policy: A Dialogue*, New York, W. W. Norton, 1969, p. 48.

89 **Federal Reserve deflation quote:** Meeting of the Federal Open Market Committee on January 29–30, 2002, p. 164.

90 **Bernanke–Mishkin quote:** Bernanke, Ben, and Frederic Mishkin, "Central Bank Behavior and the Strategy of Monetary Policy: Observations from Six Industrialized Countries," *NBER Macroeconomics Annual*, Cambridge, Mass., MIT Press, 1992.

90–91 **author's critique of Bernanke–Mishkin:** Taylor, John B., "Comment on 'Central Bank Behavior and the Strategy of Monetary Policy: Observations from Six Industrialized Countries,'" *NBER Macroeconomics Annual*, Cambridge, Mass., MIT Press, 1992.

Notes

91 Bernanke paper on Taylor curve: Bernanke, Ben, "The Great Moderation," presented at the meeting of the Eastern Economic Association, Washington, D.C., February 20, 2004.

91–92 Friedman quote: Conversation with the author.

95 timely, targeted and temporary quote: Summers, Lawrence H., "Fiscal Stimulus Issues," testimony before the Joint Economic Committee, Washington, D.C., January 16, 2008.

98 Samuelson quote: Interview with Nathan Gardels, "Don't Expect Recovery before 2012—With 8% Inflation," *New Perspectives Quarterly*, vol. 16, no. 1, Winter 2009.

99 permanent, pervasive, and predictable quote: Taylor, John B., "The State of the Economy and Principles for Fiscal Stimulus," testimony before the Committee on the Budget, United States Senate, November 19, 2008.

Chapter 3: Defusing the Debt Explosion

102 historical debt data in chart: "Historical Data on Federal Debt Held by the Public," Washington, D.C., Congressional Budget Office, July 2010.

102 future debt projections in chart: "CBO's 2010 Long-Term Budget Outlook" (alternative fiscal scenario tables), Washington, D.C., Congressional Budget Office, June 2010.

105 Douglas deficit quote: Douglas, Paul H., "The Federal Budget," *Journal of Finance*, vol. 5, no. 2, 1950, p. 147 (published version of the address given at the Joint Meeting of the American Finance Association and the American Economic Association, December 28, 1949).

Notes

112 Friedman flat tax quote: Friedman, Milton, *Capitalism and Freedom*, Chicago, University of Chicago Press, 1962, p. 174.

113 spending estimates for February 2011 budget in chart: "An Analysis of the President's Budgetary Proposals for Fiscal Year 2012," Table 1-2, Washington, D.C., Congressional Budget Office, April 2011.

113 spending estimates for Budget Control Act in chart: "Analysis of the Impact on the Deficit of the Budget Control Act of 2011 as Revised in the House," Washington, D.C., Congressional Budget Office, July 27, 2011.

Chapter 4: Monetary Rules Work and Discretion Doesn't

122 Rogoff's central banker proposal: Rogoff, Kenneth, "The Optimal Degree of Commitment to an Intermediate Monetary Target," *Quarterly Journal of Economics*, vol. 100, no. 4, 1985.

126 Taylor rule: Taylor, John B., "Discretion versus Policy Rules in Practice," *Carnegie-Rochester Series on Public Policy*, vol. 39, 1993.

128 evidence on written Fed references to dual mandate: Thornton, Daniel L., "What Does the Change in the FOMC's Statement of Objectives Mean?" Federal Reserve Bank of St. Louis, Economic Synopses, January 3, 2011.

129 Mankiw quote: Mankiw, N. Gregory, "A Mono Mandate for the Fed?" *Greg Mankiw's Blog*, December 1, 2010.

130–31 legislative history on reporting requirements: Taylor, John B., "Legislating a Rule for Monetary Policy," *Cato Journal*, vol. 31, no. 3, 2011.

Notes

133 Smets quote: Jarocinski, Marek, and Frank R. Smets, "House Prices and the Stance of Monetary Policy," *Federal Reserve Bank of St. Louis Review,* July/August 2008, p. 362.

133 Ahrend quote: Ahrend, Rüdiger, "Monetary Ease: A Factor behind Financial Crises? Some Evidence from OECD Countries," *Economics: The Open Access, Open Assessment E-Journal,* vol. 4, April 14, 2010, p. 19.

133–34 Bernanke speech criticizing author's findings: Bernanke, Ben, "Monetary Policy and the Housing Bubble," presented at the Annual Meeting of the American Economic Association, January 3, 2010.

134 author's response to Bernanke: Taylor, John B., "The Fed and the Crisis: A Reply to Ben Bernanke," *Wall Street Journal,* January 11, 2010.

135 evidence on Fed's auction facility: Taylor, John B., and John C. Williams, "A Black Swan in the Money Market," *American Economic Journal: Macroeconomics,* vol. 1, no. 1, 2009.

135–36 recommended strategy preceding the panic: Taylor, John B., "Toward a New Framework for Exceptional Access," presentation at the Policy Workshop on the Future Role of Central Banking: Urgent and Precedent-Setting Next Steps, Hoover Institution, Stanford University, Stanford, Calif., July 22, 2008.

138 research paper on mortgage-backed securities purchases: Stroebel, Johannes C., and John B. Taylor, "Estimated Impact of the Fed's Mortgage-Backed Securities Purchase Program," *International Journal of Central Banking,* in press (2012).

139–40 data for bank money chart: H.4.1 Federal Reserve statistical release (reserve balances with Federal Reserve Banks) and counterfactual calculated by the author.

Chapter 5: Ending Crony Capitalism as We Know It

152 O'Neill quote: Morgenson, Gretchen, and Joshua Rosner, *Reckless Endangerment: How Outsized Ambition, Greed, and Corruption Led to Economic Armageddon*, New York, Times Books, 2011, p. 86.

154 Ryan quote: Ryan, Paul D., "The GOP Path to Prosperity," *Wall Street Journal*, April 5, 2011.

154 Johnson quote: Johnson, Simon, "The Problem with the F.D.I.C.'s Powers," *Economix*, April 28, 2011.

158–59 Chapter 14 proposal: Jackson, Thomas, "Bankruptcy Code Chapter 14: A Proposal," Resolution Project, Economic Policy Working Group, Hoover Institution, Stanford University, Stanford, Calif., April 2011.

159–60 Shultz quote: Shultz, George P., "A Conversation about Key Conclusions," in Kenneth E. Scott, George P. Shultz, and John B. Taylor (eds.), *Ending Government Bailouts as We Know Them*, Stanford, Calif., Hoover Press, 2010.

162–63 Atlas quote: Atlas, Scott W., *In Excellent Health: Setting the American Record Straight on Health Care*, Stanford, Calif., Hoover Press, 2011, p. 233.

164 Cogan-Hubbard-Kessler quote: Cogan, John F., R. Glenn Hubbard, and Daniel P. Kessler, *Healthy, Wealthy, and Wise*, Stanford, Calif., Hoover Press, 2011, p. 41.

Chapter 6: Improving Lives While Spiking the Entitlement Explosion

167–68 data from Survey of Income and Program Participation: John F. Cogan, "Receiving Assistance from Federal Transfer Programs," Hoover Institution, Working Paper, December 20, 2010.

Notes

170 **future Social Security and federal health projections in chart:** "CBO's 2010 Long-Term Budget Outlook" (alternative fiscal scenario tables), Washington, D.C., Congressional Budget Office, June 2010.

173 **Ryan Medicare proposal:** "The Path to Prosperity: Restoring America's Promise," Fiscal Year 2012 Budget Resolution, passed out of House Budget Committee, April 6, 2011.

173 **Obama Medicare proposal:** "The President's Framework for Shared Prosperity and Shared Fiscal Responsibility, Fact Sheet," White House, Office of the Press Secretary, April 13, 2011.

175 **evidence of imaging overpayments:** Winter, Ariel, and Nancy Ray, "Paying Accurately for Imaging Services in Medicare," *Health Affairs*, vol. 27, no. 6, 2008.

176 **rationing cataract operations in Britain's National Health Service (NHS):** Wright, Oliver, "Cataracts, Hips, Knees and Tonsils: NHS Begins Rationing Operations," *The Independent*, July 28, 2011.

181 **golden rule reform:** "Social Security Policy Options," Option 17, Washington, D.C., Congressional Budget Office, July 2010.

182 **Shultz-Shoven quote:** Shultz, George P., and John B. Shoven with Matthew Gunn and Gopi Shah Goda, *Putting Our House in Order: A Guide to Social Security and Health Care Reform*, New York, W. W. Norton, 2008, pp. 40, 44.

185 **CBO report on income distribution**: "Trends in the Distribution of Household Income Between 1979 and 2007," Washington, D.C., Congressional Budget Office, October 2011.

Chapter 7: Rebuilding American Economic Leadership

186 **students' reaction to Geithner speech in China:** Conway, Edmund, "Geithner Insists Chinese Dollar Assets Are Safe," *Telegraph* (UK), June 1, 2009.

193–94 **setting up Iraq's financial system:** Taylor, John B., *Global Financial Warriors: The Untold Story of International Finance in the Post-9/11 World*, New York, W. W. Norton, 2007.

194 **Geithner June 2010 letter to G20:** Letter from Timothy F. Geithner, June 3, 2010, available at http://online.wsj.com/public/resources/documents/Geithnerletter0604.PDF.

195 **quote from G20 in June 2010:** Communiqué from meeting of finance ministers and central bank governors in Busan, Korea, June 5, 2010.

195 **quote from G20 in October 2011:** Communiqué from meeting of finance ministers and central bank governors in Paris, France, October 14–15, 2011.

196 **Schäuble quote:** Evans-Pritchard, Ambrose, "Germany Slams 'Stupid' US Plans to Boost EU Rescue Fund," *Telegraph* (UK), September 27, 2011.

196 **economists' letter to the G8:** Jouini, Elyès, "G8 Support for a Tunisian Plan," *Huffington Post*, May 19, 2011.

197 **Nabli quote:** Nabli, Mustapha, *Breaking the Barriers to Higher Economic Growth: Better Governance and Deeper Reforms in the Middle East and North Africa*, Washington, D.C., World Bank, 2008, online abstract, available at http://www–wds.worldbank.org/external/default/WDSContentServer/WDSP/IB/2008/05/30/000334955_20080530063805/Rendered/PDF/439690PUB0Box310only109780821374153.pdf.

199 quotes from the Riksbank discussion: "Minutes of the Executive Board's Monetary Policy Meeting, No. 4," Sveriges Riksbank, Stockholm, September 1, 2010, p. 12.

200 evidence on impact of low Fed interest rate on European Central Bank interest rate: Taylor, John B., "Globalization and Monetary Policy: Missions Impossible," in Mark Gertler and Jordi Gali (eds.), *The International Dimension of Monetary Policy*, Chicago, University of Chicago Press, 2009.

201 evidence on impact of the low European Central Bank interest rate on Greece, Ireland, and Spain: Ahrend, Rüdiger, Boris Cournede, and Robert Price, "Monetary Policy, Market Excesses, and Financial Turmoil," OECD Economics Working Paper No. 597, Paris, Organisation for Economic Co-operation and Development, March 2008.

203 U.S. Treasury work on Chinese currency: Taylor, John B., *Global Financial Warriors: The Untold Story of International Finance in the Post-9/11 World*, New York, W. W. Norton, 2007.

203–4 Chinese intervention with Wal-Mart: Bussey, John, "China: Bullying to Prosperity," *Wall Street Journal*, October 14, 2011.

Index

Page numbers in *italics* refer to graphs.

Index

Index

Index

Index

impact of U.S. financial policies on, 201–2

move toward rule-based economic policies in, 122, 193

Ending Government Bailouts as We Know Them (Scott, Shultz, and Taylor), 159–60

entitlement programs:
as disincentives, 168, 171–72
government spending on, 168–71, *170*
purpose of, 167–68
reform of, 10, 117, 166–85
tax rates and, 183–85
see also specific programs

environmental policy, 20, 145

Environmental Protection Agency (EPA), 145

Erdoğan, Recep, 193

Europe:
Central and Eastern, 191, 196, 197
2011 financial crisis in, 107, 201

European Central Bank, 122, 133

Eurozone, interest rates in, 200

exchange rates, 189, 190, 202–3

Face the Nation, 80

"Failure of Financial Reform, Itemized, The" (Talbott), 153

Fannie Mae, 148, 149–50, 151–52, 157

"Federal Budget, The" (Douglas), 105

Federal Deposit Insurance Corporation, 137–38, 148

orderly liquidation authority of, 155–56, 159–60

Federal Housing Finance Agency (FHFA), 148

Federal Housing Finance Board, 148

Federal Open Market Committee, 32–33, 89

Federal Reserve, 58, 78–81, 89, 97, 148, 154
accountability of, 32–33, 130–39, 142–43
bank money created by, 139–41, *140*
dual mandate of, 124–26, 128, 138–39
fiscal policy as properly outside purview of, 123–24
foreign central banks as influenced by, 198–201
independence of, 65, 122, 142
inflation and, 73–74, 79–80, 94–95, 124–25, 141, 142
interest rates set by, 34–35, 43, 44, 65, 78–81, 88, 121, 126, 127–28, 129, 131, 132–33
see also interest rates "too low for too long"
interventionist policies of, 29–30, 34–35, 43, 45–46, 65–67, 127–29, 134–43, 187, 190
as lender of last resort, 126, 137
mortgage-backed securities bought by, 37, 128, 138–39, 141
predictability and, 30–31, 32–33, 45, 88, 121–22, 135–43

Index

Index

Index

Index

Macroeconomic Advisers, 118
macroeconomics, 28
Madigan, Brian, 83
Major, John, 191
Mankiw, Greg, 129
market system, 11, 16, 18, 19, 21, 22, 27, 33, 62, 78, 98, 107, 146, 164, 174
Martin, William McChesney, 65–66, 73, 81, 92
Mazowiecki, Tadeusz, 193
McCain, John, 96
McCracken, Paul, 67, 71
Medicaid, 167
  government spending on, 117, 169–71, *170*
  reform of, 163–64, 166, 177–79
Medicare, 168
  government spending on, 117, 169–71, *170*
  Part D of, 174
  payroll tax, 184–85
  reduced payment rates of, 176
  reform of, 164, 172–77, 178, 183
Medicare Payment Advisory Commission, 175
Meltzer, Allan, 47, 66, 73, 130
mercantilism, 20
Mexico, 187
Meyer, Laurence, 118
Middle East and North Africa (MENA), 194
  economic freedom and, 196–97
  political awakenings in, 188
  U.S. promotion of interventionism in, 196–97
Miller, G. William, 78
Mishkin, Frederic, 90

MIT (Massachusetts Institute of Technology), Economics Department at, 59
monetary aggregates, 130–31
Monetary History of the United States, A (Friedman and Schwartz), 47
monetary policy, 10, 44, 62, 77, 121–43, 197
  Congress and, 123, 125, 143
  coordination of fiscal policy and, 66
  economic freedom and, 25
  inflation as focus of, 32, 88, 121, 125
  interventionism in, 26, 28, 29–30, 34–35, 46, 61, 66, 97, 121, 189, 190, 191
  money supply in, 29, 32, 37, 43, 45, 48, 65, 69, 89, 93, 121, 126, 128–29, 130–31, 139–41, *140,* 154, 190, 201
  necessity of clear goals in, 123
  price stability as focus of, 31, 93–94, 121, 125–28, 142
  quantitative easing in, 37, 43, 45, 93, 128–29, 141, 201
  of Reagan, 78–81
  rules-based approach to, 82–84, 91, 121, 129–32, 142–43
  2008 financial crisis and, 37
  unemployment as focus of, 32
  see also Federal Reserve; fiscal policy; policy rules
money-market funds, 36, 46, 137–38
Moody's Analytics, 118
moral hazard, 160

Index

Morgenson, Gretchen, 151–52
Morocco, 194
mortgage-backed securities, 37, 128, 138–39, 141, 149
Mozilo, Angelo, 152

Nabli, Mustapha, 197
national debt, 46, 101–20
    deficits and, 104
    and failure to apply principles of economic freedom, 101, 106–7
    interest payments on, 107, 117
    percentage of GDP to, *see* debt ratio
    surpluses and, 104
national defense, 20, 26
National Economic Council, 97
National Health Service, British, 176
National Industrial Recovery Act (NIRA; 1933), 48, 49
National Security Council, 192
Newsweek, 68, 69
Nixon, Richard, 28, 73, 81
    free-market pronouncements of, 67
    interventionist policies of, 59, 68–72
    wage and price freeze of, 29, 44, 69, 70–71
    Watergate scandal and, 72
Norges Bank, 198, 199
North Africa, *see* Middle East and North Africa
Norway, 198

Obama, Barack, 93, 96, 114, 187, 194, 196

health care reform of, *see* Patient Protection and Affordable Care Act
interventionist policies of, 84, 97–99, 195
Medicare reform plan of, 173–77, 178, 183
2009 stimulus package of, 97
2011 budget plan of, 113–15
Office of Federal Housing Enterprise Oversight (OHFEO), 148
Office of the Comptroller of the Currency, 148, 157
Office of Thrift Supervision, 157
Ohanian, Lee, 48
oil shock, 65
Oman, 194
O'Neill, June, 152
O'Neill, Paul, 85–87, 94
Operation Twist, 66, 93, 190, 201
Organisation for Economic Co-operation and Development, 122, 133, 200

Papola, John, 144*n*
patents, 21
Patient Protection and Affordable Care Act (2010), 37, 39, 145, 147, 164
    disincentives in, 171–72
    economic freedom violated by, 160–62
    insurance mandates in, 161–62
Paulson, Hank, 94–95, 137
payday loans, 156
Personal Responsibility and Work Opportunity Reconciliation Act (PRWORA; 1996), 177

Index

Index

Index